ESTRENO Collection of Contemporary Spanish Plays

General Editor: Phyllis Zatlin

PACKING UP THE PAST

SEBASTIÁN JUNYENT

PACKING UP THE PAST

(Hay que deshacer la casa)

Translated by Ana Mengual

ESTRENO Plays
New Brunswick, New Jersey
2000

ESTRENO Contemporary Spanish Plays 18
General Editor: Phyllis Zatlin
              Department of Spanish & Portuguese
              Faculty of Arts & Sciences
              Rutgers, The State University of New Jersey
              105 George Street
              New Brunswick, NJ 08901-1414 USA

Library of Congress Cataloging-in-Publication Data
Junyent, Sebastián, 1948
    Packing up the Past.
    Translation of: Hay que deshacer la casa.
    Contents: Packing up the Past.
    1. Junyent, Sebastián, 1948. Translation, English.
I. Mengual, Ana. II. Title
Library of Congress Catalog Card No.: 99-71173
ISBN: 1-888463-10-4

© 2000 Copyright by ESTRENO Plays

Original Play © Sebastián Junyent, 1985.
English Translation © Ana Mengual, 2000
First Edition

All rights reserved.
Except for brief passages quoted in newspapers, magazines, radio or television, no part of this publication may be reproduced or transmitted in any form or by any means, electronic or mechanical, including photocopy, recording, or by an information storage and retrieval system, without permission in writing from the publisher.

Published with support from
Program for Cultural Cooperation between
Spain's Ministry of Education and Culture
and United States' Universities

Cover: Jeffrey Eads

A NOTE ON *PACKING UP THE PAST*

Ostensibly, *Packing up the Past* is a simple story of two sisters, separated for many years by time and space, coming together to settle the affairs of their family home. The older and dutiful sister Laura, married with children, has spent most of her life between her parents and her "new" family. The younger Ana, a sort of prodigal daughter who ran away at age seventeen, returns only after the deaths of both mother and father. The title refers both to the sisters "packing up the house" as well as to those memories, both good and painful, that have to be faced once again before they can also be packed away.

However simple the play may seem at the surface, it floats on strong undercurrents of conflict and change. The house is in a small Spanish provincial town that is caught between traditional old world Catholicism and new ideas and ways. The play takes place in a time period that is segueing between the old political system dominated by Franco and the modern political picture. The two sisters, raised in the traditional male-dominated social structure are having to deal with choices they made in their pasts that are now affecting their options for the future.

There are more than just the two characters in the play, though. First, there is the house itself. It is not just the setting for the play, but a refuge for Laura from her dead-end marriage, a hesitant homecoming for Ana and a prison that houses memories for both. There are also all the artifacts the sisters go through that bring back many recollections of childlike innocence as well as of pain. And then there is the father, once such a dominating figure, now only a portrait, but a portrait that still not only commands but demands his presence.

The play then becomes a negotiation of sorts. Both sisters discuss, argue and even at one point gamble for the material objects left by their parents. But the negotiation goes far deeper. As they go through the process of sorting everything, they are confronted with their pasts. Each confrontation reveals more and more about the characters, both to themselves and to us. The negotiation becomes then, not over material goods, but for identity, freedom and happiness. What both sisters finally obtain through this negotiation is a mixture of what they want, what they need and what they are afraid to face.

Toward the end of the play Ana and Laura try to make sense of their lives and what has happened to them during the course of the long afternoon. Laura says, "This afternoon must have been good for something." Ana replies, "For us to realize that nothing changes. . . not us. . . not our lives. We're the same ignorant, scared little girls that played in this house. We've only gained in years and disillusionment. We'll both try to forget this afternoon. It'll always be the afternoon we packed up the house." Laura looks around at the surroundings and finally says,

Packing up the Past, Converse College, Spartanburg, South Carolina, May 2000. Directed by Steven R. Hunt and featuring Erin Flynn and Sarah Ibarra in the roles of Ana and Laura.

"You mean the afternoon we destroyed it." Yes, in a sense, they have destroyed the house. But as in Chekhov, there must be some destruction in order for growth In the end, Ana goes back to Madrid to her new husband with a promise that she and her sister will see each other again. Laura decides to stay the night in the empty house rather than face the "emptiness" of her loveless "new" home. But despite the unsettling conclusion to *Packing up the Past*, one is left with a sense that these two women have finally accomplished something, if only a beginning.

Packing up the Past takes place in Spain and has several topical references to specific political and social situations. However, the essential dramatic ingredient is relationship; specifically the relationship between the two sisters and collectively between the women and their family. The important word here is "character". The play is about two human beings in a special situation that is critical and crucial to their own individual needs. All this adds up to drama enhanced. The result is that the play relates to all women of all cultures, as well as being an interesting piece of theatre to all audiences, male or female.

                                                    Steven R. Hunt
                                                    Assistant Professor of Theatre
                                                    Converse College

SEBASTIÁN JUNYENT
Photo: Phyllis Zatlin

ABOUT THE PLAYWRIGHT

Sebastián Junyent (b. Madrid, 1948) is an important figure in Spanish theatre and television. In 1966, he began his career as an actor; he appeared, primarily as a comic actor, in stage plays, movies, and television. As an author, his earliest plays were written for café-theatre, starting in 1970. In the past decade, he has written scripts and directed numerous, highly successful series and specials for Telecinco and TVE. Despite his time-consuming commitment to television work, he continues to write for the stage, and it is in this area that he has achieved international acclaim. Junyent's best-known plays, which have been performed throughout Spain and abroad, include *Hay que deshacer la casa* (*Packing up the Past*, 1985), *Señora de...* (Mrs..., 1987), *Gracias abuela* (Thank You, Grandma, 1990), and *Solo, solo para mujeres* (Just for Women, 1993). While the subject matter and tone vary, his theatre generally takes what might be considered a feminist perspective on the role of women in contemporary society. His plays are often marked by surface humor, as well as psychological and sociological insights.

Junyent's major stage play to date is the one chosen for this ESTRENO edition: *Packing up the Past*. This two-character play was winner of the prestigious Lope de Vega prize for 1983 and premiered with a stellar cast: Amparo Rivelles and Lola Cardona. It played to full houses at Madrid's Teatro de la Comedia from January to June, 1985, when it closed to go on tour to Miami. It subsequently returned to Madrid, with the original cast, to the Teatro Fígaro, where it ran through a second year. A critical as well as box office success, the original production garnered many prizes in 1985 for the author and the actresses, including the Premio Espectador y la Crítica for Rivelles and Cardona. The play has been televised, made into a movie, and performed widely throughout Spain and Spanish America, in Spanish at Hispanic theatres in the U.S. and Canada, and, in translation, in Brazil, France, Italy, and Turkey.

Phyllis Zatlin

CAUTION: Professionals and amateurs are hereby warned that *Packing up the Past,* being fully protected under the Copyright Laws of the United States of America, the British Empire, including the Dominion of Canada, and all other countries covered by the Pan-American Copyright Convention and the Universal Copyright Conventions, and of all countries with which the United States has reciprocal copyright relations, is subject to royalty. All rights, including professional, amateur, motion picture, recitation, public reading, radio and television broadcasting, and the rights of translation into foreign languages, are strictly reserved. Particular emphasis is laid on the question of readings, permission for which must be secured in writing.

Inquiries regarding permissions should be addressed directly to the author through

Alfredo Carrión Sáiz
Director de Artes Escénicas y Musicales
Sociedad General de Autores y Editores
Fernando VI, 4
28004 Madrid, SPAIN
Phone: 011-34-91-349 96 86   Fax: 011-34-91-349 97 12
E-mail: acarrion@sgae.es

or through the translator:

Ana Mengual
1388 2nd Avenue, Apt. 3A
New York, NY 10021
Phone: 1-212-734-7134
E-mail: ana_mengual@hotmail.com

Hay que deshacer la casa (Packing up the Past) was winner of the Lope de Vega prize for 1983. It was first performed at the Teatro Principal of Valencia on 28 December 1984 and opened in Madrid, at the Teatro de la Comedia, on 17 January 1985. Directed by Joaquín Vida, the production starred Amparo Rivelles and Lola Cardona.

The play was first performed in Spanish in the United States, in Miami, in June 1985, with the original cast.

Packing up the Past received its American premiere at Converse College in Spartanburg, South Carolina on 10 May 2000, directed by Steven R. Hunt.

A FRIENDLY LETTER TO THOSE WHO STAGE THIS WORK

Dear Colleagues,

We playwrights usually address you through the impersonality of stage directions. This time I'd like to communicate my wishes and ideas to you more directly and personally. Above all, I want to thank you for the confidence you have put in my words and your courage in bringing them to the stage. In all modesty, I'd like to tell you that what I have written is what I wanted to say, and nothing more. So don't go crazy looking for underlying meanings that don't exist.

My story merely relates two people's encounter: their memories, their hopes, their love. It also tells how people feel who are dragging their own cadaver, without even knowing how or when they died.

As you can see, I've told the plot. I did so for two reasons: first, to make my intentions clear in case I did not get them across and you have to clarify them through your actions. The second reason is in case the work isn't staged. Once the plot is told, at least the critic's work will be done, since that is the specialty of the critic in our country. I think we should call them advance men.

To the actresses who are in the play, I only have one thing to say: use the text as an outline. Substitute some of your own words, which will always be more in sync with your feelings than what I have written. And use your memories if the ones I have created are not enough.

To the director, go ahead and cut, summarize, expand, substitute and clarify as you wish, as long as you do it lovingly. Don't worry about possible complaints from the author. I leave my text to those who must face the public on a daily basis.

To hell with drama to be read! Drama is for the person who performs it or watches it, not for the one who sits and reads it with his imagination turned off.

As for how the play should be performed, it will suffice for all to do it with great feeling and for the actresses to have the right look. Their hands will always be working, but not gesturing in the worst sense of the word.

And that is all, my dear colleagues, thank you and. . . break a leg!

The Author

CHARACTERS

LAURA
ANA, her sister, who is four or five years younger.

ACTION

Continuous, during the course of a single afternoon. The action unfolds in a large old house in a small Spanish town featuring characters from today's Spain, in collaboration with all the old familiar Spanish ghosts.

SET

    I don't care whether it's realistic or merely suggested. That's your problem and the problem of the budget, as long as there are boxes, knickknacks, books and papers all over the stage. We also need the portrait of a rather severe looking man dressed formally. The portrait should be rigged so we can bust it up over and over at every show. Oh, I almost forgot! We need a chair or some kind of couch for resting the buns on once in a while. I don't ask for much, so I don't want to hear it from those people who run around saying it's impossible to stage the works of Spanish authors.
    When the action begins, the whole set should look like a house which is being dismantled or packed up. Papers, pictures, books, and a bunch of empty or full boxes should help create this effect. There should also be some old fashioned candelabra with candles spread about the room, which is the living room of this old large house. There are two doors, one opening towards the inner rooms; the other, which is slightly ajar, reveals the light of a stairwell to the street. The room is dimly lit. The only real light comes from the half-open door we just mentioned and from the large wall facing the audience where we imagine there to be two large windows. The windows are not visible to the audience, but rather suggested by the motions of the actresses and the talent of the lighting crew. Another point of light originates from behind one of the semi-drawn curtains that we assume are on the imaginary windows.

2- Sebastián Junyent

In the hallway, we see ANA. She knocks on the door, finds it open and walks in. She tries to turn on the switch, but the light doesn't work. She stumbles over a number of objects until she reaches the first window. She opens the curtain and in pours the bright light of the afternoon sun. She turns and looks around the room.

ANA: Laura! Laura!

(Since there is no answer, she walks to the second window and draws open the curtains. The light remains steady. She walks to the inner door and knocks again, then leaves the stage. We hear her voice off. She then reappears and stops in front of the portrait, shrinks away from it, takes out a cigarette and lights it. She unbuttons her coat, sits, gets up, walks around, and finally finds the old rotary telephone on the wall and dials.)

ANA: Carlos? Hi, I'm here. No, I haven't seen her yet. She must have gone out for a minute. The door was open. . .What? Bad. . . I feel really bad. This whole thing makes me very uncomfortable. As soon as I see her, I'm leaving. . . I know what I'm doing. . . I don't care! Yes. Anyway, there's a train leaving in an hour, so I'll probably be on it. Don't worry, I'll let you know if I change my mind, but I doubt it. Listen, don't forget to pick up the coat at the cleaners, the ticket is on the night stand. No, wait, I put it on the hall table. . . All right. Then I'd call you, Okay? Bye.

(She hangs up and once again starts walking around the room, glancing at the objects. She then approaches one of the windows and decides to open it. The noise of the street--cars and voices--rises. She immediately closes the window and remains behind the glass.)

(We see LAURA, who appears at the outer door. She is wearing an elegant fur coat and is holding some packages---food and drink. She can tell by the increased light in the room that ANA has arrived and looks around for her. She puts down the packages.)

LAURA: Ana!

(She moves toward her. They look at each other for a moment and then hug. ANA breaks the embrace.)

ANA: I figured you would be here soon since the door was unlocked.

LAURA: I was sure you'd come. I just had to run out to the store, so I left the door open. What train did you take? You have no idea how happy I am to see you here. *(She takes off her coat and puts it on a chair.)*
ANA: I took the two o'clock train... Laura, I...
LAURA *(Taking a sample of dust with her finger)*: Ugh, this is filthy. I'm going to go change. I'll put on my cleaning clothes. Do you want to change, too?
ANA: No, thanks. Listen... I...
LAURA: I'll be right back! *(As she exits.)* Go look for some cups. They must be in one of these boxes. There's some fresh coffee in the thermos... a cup of coffee will give us a little pickup. It's very cold outside.
ANA *(Hesitant, she finally starts looking. She looks through the boxes and finds some cups. She stares at them)*: I found the ones from the set of dishes. They look clean.
LAURA *(Offstage)*: Yes, I washed them before I put them away. I'm still a clean freak. You have no idea how I've been slaving for the past few days. Everything had been let go for so long. *(She appears wearing some kind of robe or housecoat. She has taken off her heels and is wearing slippers.)* The thermos is over here. *(She takes out the thermos and pours some coffee.)* Would you like something to eat?
ANA: No, thanks. Just coffee'll be fine.
LAURA *(Making room so they can sit next to each other)*: Wait a minute. My goodness, look at all this junk! I was hoping you'd come. There is too much stuff here for just me to deal with. Now that you're here, it'll make everything easier.
ANA: That's what I wanted to talk to you about. As soon as I finish my coffee, I'm leaving.
LAURA: What? You're leaving? Are you crazy? What about the house? And all this stuff? There's a ton of things here that have to be taken care of. You can't leave. I won't let you leave after you've finally deigned to show up.
ANA: It was silly of me to come. It hit me the moment I walked through the door. I can't stand this house. I feel sick.
LAURA: And how do you think I feel? You may as well stay since you're already here. It's better to face things right away. You can't put them off forever.
ANA: I'm not asking you to put anything off. I'm just asking you to let me leave and then you can take care of things anyway you want. I have nothing to do with this place.
LAURA: Of course you do! It was Mother's wish! She's the one who decided we would be equals.
ANA: Well, to hell with Mother's wishes. I'm out of here!

LAURA: Wait... calm down... listen to me! It's just as unpleasant for me as it is for you to have to stay here to deal with all this. I want to leave too, but someone's got to do it. I'm sick of always being the one who gets stuck doing everything. You're back in Spain now. You've had the strength to take the train and make it this far, now all you have to do is hang in there a little longer. A few more hours and it'll all be over. So get ready to do some work because you're staying... whether you like it or not.

ANA: Is that an order?

LAURA: It's a plea. The least you could do is help me this time... I deserve it. Please, Ana. I'm not asking for much... just a few hours. If we hurry you can get back to Madrid tonight.

ANA: It's just that I don't know what you expect us to do here. When you called me you said, "We have to pack up the house," and I... I don't really know what that's supposed to mean.

LAURA: You mean to tell me that after all the traveling you've done all over the world you don't know what it means to pack up a house?

ANA: I've never packed a house up. I've always lived in small apartments. Leaving an apartment isn't the same. It's not closing up.

LAURA: It's the same thing. Closing up, leaving, packing, getting rid of, renting, selling, giving away. It's all the same. It's still parting with something. Sometimes you're happy to do it, but other times it's unpleasant, like today.

ANA: Well, **you** pack, **you** sell, **you** give away, **you** rent, but don't count on me for any of it.

LAURA: If it were up to me, I can assure you, I wouldn't have counted on you for anything. It wouldn't have been that hard. I've been making decisions on my own for years. But this time it's different. There are financial concerns. Things that have to be divided up. There are papers. There are Father's things, Mother's things, your things. I can't decide for both of us. Besides, Mother wanted us to do it together.

ANA *(Looking at the collection of objects)*: And how am I supposed to know what to do with all this stuff? I don't even know what half of these things are. I've been away for so many years... it's all strange to me.

LAURA: Are you sure? Come on, pick something up... anything. Tell me, is this strange to you? This? Nothing that's here can be strange to you. It's our past... they're our things.

ANA: They were our things. They had their value at the time... now they're worthless. All we have left is time...

LAURA: A minute ago you said you felt bad from the moment you stepped into this house. If it were all strange to you, you wouldn't feel anything. You have to be strong and face up to things for once in your life. I don't

Packing up the Past-5

think it's too much to ask. I know this must be hard for you to come back after all this time and find everything a mess. It's very unpleasant. . . but you have no choice. Finish your coffee. We have a lot of work to do. *(Rummaging through some papers.)* Look, your old report card! *(She hands it to her.)* Who knows if you might need it for something?

ANA *(Glancing quickly)*: At this stage of the game?

LAURA *(Showing her a picture)*: Look what I found. . . your grade school pictures!

ANA: I don't want to see anything. Don't you understand that none of this means anything to me? Too much has happened in my life since I last saw this living room. Only. . . only Father's portrait. . . that damned portrait always scared me. It still has the same effect.

LAURA: You'd be shocked if you saw this picture. You would see what time can do to a cute little girl with blond hair.

ANA *(Taking the picture)*: I couldn't have looked that cute. I remember I was missing a tooth and didn't even want to have it taken.

LAURA *(Looking at the picture with her)*: You were adorable. I can't believe how Mother and I struggled with those braids of yours.

ANA: And I had it taken. You remember how impossible Sister Agnes was.

LAURA *(Imitating her voice)*: Pictures are required, girls. We make them a requirement because none of you should miss the opportunity to have a lovely remembrance of your childhood.

ANA *(Mimicking the same voice)*: Your parents will have to pay seven cents for each picture. If you want copies for your grandparents, tell your parents they're five cents apiece.

LAURA: And you posed for it. . . pouting, but you did it. Look at the map! Prussia!

ANA *(Slowly ripping up her picture)*: That enormous blotch of color will still always be Prussia to those nuns. It took me fifteen years to realize Prussia didn't exist anymore.

LAURA: Why did you rip it up? I saved mine. You could have given it to me. Yoli would have loved to keep it. She loves old things.

ANA: Yoli? Your daughter Yolanda. . . But she's only seen me once. . . six years ago.

LAURA: She completely idolizes you. She says her parents, we're reactionaries, but you, you're the "with it" aunt. . . the embodiment of freedom.

ANA: Obviously, she doesn't know me very well. What's she like?

LAURA: She looks a lot like. . .

ANA: I asked you what she's like, not who she looks like.

Packing Up the Past, Real Coliseo de Carlos III, El Escorial, September 1985. Directed by Joaquín Vida. Amparo Rivelles and Lola Cardona as Laura and Ana. Photo by Manuel Martínez Muñoz.

LAURA: Well, she's... she's like Dad in a lot of ways. I can't really explain without giving you a specific example. She's very demanding... very intense. The boy is different. He's more carefree. Things don't bother him as much.
ANA: Then he's not like anybody in our family. How old is he?
LAURA: Seventeen... a difficult age.
ANA: All ages are difficult. I left home at that age. Centuries ago...
LAURA: Can you help me with this box?
ANA: It weighs a ton. What's in here?
LAURA: Dad's books. The good ones... the leather bound ones. I put them away immediately so they wouldn't get scratched up. Look through them. You can keep them all. Antonio has a huge library, but there's no room left for anything more.
ANA *(Looking at the books)*: His old dictionary! Do you remember when we used to look up words?
LAURA: Words that gave other words as definitions and so it got more and more confusing.
ANA: Whore... prostitute... harlot. Woman given to indiscriminate lewdness for hire. What does she hire? Does she sell it? Rent it? It was impossible to make any sense of it, but at least we learned new words. *(Pause.)* Maybe I'll keep a book or two. Dad had some really interesting ones. I still love books. With time they've become an obsession.
LAURA: You used to spend hours reading. Mother always said you would be a writer.
ANA: But I wanted to be a doctor. In the end, I'm neither. I work as a librarian.
LAURA: A librarian? You never mentioned it when we spoke on the phone.
ANA: I haven't been working that long and it's still not permanent. I'm in charge of issuing cards at a public library.
LAURA: Do you enjoy it?
ANA: No, but the money comes in handy, at least until Carlos finds a job. It's harder for him since he's not a citizen.
LAURA: I only met him the day you arrived. He seemed very nice... very sweet. Maybe it was the accent. What does he do?
ANA: In Chile he was a lawyer, but when we were living in Paris, after going into exile, he worked in whatever he could find. He'll probably have to do the same now.
LAURA: Is he a communist too?
ANA: Too? Who else do you have in mind?
LAURA: Oh, come on, Ana! Juan was a communist.
ANA: No, neither one is a communist.
LAURA: But Juan... his ideas...

8- Sebastián Junyent

ANA: I don't think he had too many ideas. And the few he did have were not communist, I can assure you.
LAURA: Have you heard from him?
ANA: No. . . I'm going to call Carlos. If I have to stay, I'll let him know not to wait up for me. *(She walks towards the phone.)*
LAURA: I'll give you some privacy if you'd like.
ANA: No, there's no need. I'll only be a minute. *(She dials.)* Hi, it's me again. Don't expect me. . . I'm staying the whole day. . . No. . . Yes. . . Okay. No, I promise. Of course. . . tonight. . . I'll take the last train. Don't worry. Besides, I don't know what time it leaves. . .Okay. . ..Don't forget to pick that up. . . See you tomorrow. *(She hangs up and proceeds to take off her coat.)*
LAURA: Don't you want to stay overnight?
ANA: Not for anything in the world! Besides, I have to go to work tomorrow. We have to hurry and finish all this. I only have a few hours to assume my role as heiress.
LAURA: You'll see, you won't regret it. It's been so long since we've spent some time together. Just the two of us. . . just like when Mom and Dad would go out and we'd be left in charge of the house. . .
ANA: Where do we start?
LAURA: You should change. You're going to get filthy with all this mess. Must be an old dress of Mother's around here someplace.
ANA *(Quickly)*: No! No. . . never mind. This is fine, don't worry about it.
LAURA: I'm going to finish putting the silverware away. If you want you can look through the linens. They're in this box. They're very old, but maybe you could use some of them. Look them over and throw away whatever you can't use.
ANA: I'll see what I can do.
LAURA: That's nice. . . he wanted to pick you up at the train station. *(Points toward the phone.)*
ANA: Who? Oh, my husband. . .
LAURA *(Cutting her off)*: You got married?
ANA: Yes, in Paris a year ago. . . These tablecloths are so old, they couldn't take another washing.
LAURA: Forget the tablecloths! How could you get married without even telling us?
ANA: Why? We were married by the Justice of the Peace. . . it was a mere formality that made it easier for us to move to Spain. Mother wouldn't have been happy.
LAURA: How do you know? I'm sure she would have gone. She would have asked me to take her. I'll never understand your damned independence.

Packing up the Past-9

ANA: I didn't think you'd care. We haven't written to each other much in the past few years. Besides, if you had come it would have unleashed a series of events that I wouldn't have known how to handle... We can definitely throw out everything in this box. It wouldn't even do for rags. What else? Can I help you with that?

LAURA: No, I'm almost done. But look, there's a pile of papers in that folder over there, next to the report cards... certificates and that kind of thing. Why don't you start looking through them and take what's yours? I'll organize the rest some other time.

ANA *(Works in silence. After a long pause)*: They baptized me in the old church, didn't they?

LAURA: Of course they did, both of us. It probably says it right there. Why?

ANA: Just curious. I've thought about that a lot lately. What's the church like? It's probably falling apart.

LAURA: Not really. The town has taken it over and they're renovating it. Even the organ works. Sometimes a man from Belgium gives beautiful concerts there. Antonio and I went to one last summer... it was wonder...

ANA: How is Antonio?

LAURA: He's doing really well... if it wasn't for the uric acid. But when he watches his diet...

ANA: I mean his personality. My last memory of him is a kid with knickers and a face full of pimples... oh, and was he serious! Remember? You always used to say he looked like a scared rabbit.

LAURA: Well, as you know, I ended up marrying the rabbit. He's still just as serious, except he doesn't wear knickers or have pimples anymore. He's a strong person, very strict with the children, very sure of himself and always very tied up in his business. I can't say he's been my dream man, but I have no complaints. What about you? Are you happy with Carlos?

ANA: Are you...?

LAURA *(Chiding)*: "It is impolite to..."

ANA *(Going along with her)*: "Answer a question with another question..."

LAURA: You still remember!

ANA: I always have Father's sayings stirring around in here. *(Points to her head, of course.)* And he would always repeat that. I've hated being questioned ever since I was a child. I've always avoided interrogations. Father must have noticed.

LAURA: He was a wonderful man.

ANA: You still believe that? I always thought he was horrible. He used to scare me.

LAURA: You? Don't be silly. You were the only person who ever knew how to stand up to him.

ANA: You're wrong. I never managed to stand up to him. Not even a minute ago. When I walked in here and saw his portrait, I was afraid. The same way I was afraid of him back then. Damned fear. . . that's why I left home.
LAURA: You left because you were in love with Juan.
ANA: Juan was the excuse I used to get out of here, that's all.
LAURA: In your letter you said you were in love and that you were running away with him because you were head over heels. I'm sure you weren't lying.
ANA: No, I wasn't lying. I was young and I thought I was in love. It was a challenge. . . running away at seventeen with a thirty-year-old man who was divorced.
LAURA: Separated!
ANA: You're right, separated. That made it an even bigger scandal. A romantic adventure I jumped into head first in an attempt to get away from this house.
LAURA: My hair still stands on end when I remember Father reading your letter.
ANA: I can imagine the scene they made. It must have been wonderfully melodramatic.
LAURA (*Wiping a fork*): No. Actually it was rather sad. Dad read the letter and without a word, started to cry--first in silence, then gasping and screaming, his arms around Mother's waist. Once he started to calm down, he stayed in his armchair, crushed, unable to move. He was pitiful. I was surprised. It was the first time I had ever seen Dad cry and it gave me a strange feeling. . . it bordered on disgust. Mother and I, we had to carry him to bed between the two of us. I stopped respecting him that day. He had always been so strong, so tough. To me, Dad had always been a combination of Spencer Tracy and Humphrey Bogart, you know? And that day. . . well, the silverware's ready now. What have you found there?
ANA: Some certificates and my high school diploma. I'll take them, maybe they'll be useful for something. . . I find what you just told me hard to believe. I can't picture the illustrious lawyer crying.
LAURA: You're being unfair, talking about him like that. He was deeply hurt.
ANA: You could be right. . . you probably are. You were always more sensible than I was.
LAURA: Are you being sarcastic?
ANA: No, don't pay any attention to me. I've been very ironic lately. It's a habit, must come with age. . . Oh my God! It's Luis! Why aren't you saving his picture?

Packing up the Past-11

LAURA: Let me see! *(Laughing.)* Little Luis on his First Communion day! Do you remember how we used to fight over him? We were both so in love! When he walked out of the church we were both outside waiting for him.
ANA: Our knees knocking to see which one of us he would say hello to first, wearing those huge coats Aunt Susana bought us.
LAURA: They were bright red. . . with growing room. Back then they bought everything with growing room and nothing ever fit the way it was supposed to. When we first wore something, it was too big and by the following year, it was too small.
ANA: But at least we got to wear things that were new. Remember the Diaz sisters who always got hand me downs? *(Referring to the picture.)* He was adorable when he was little. He looked like an angel with all those blond curls. Is he still in India?
LAURA: He died two years ago, right after Father.
ANA: How did he die?
LAURA: Can you believe it! His whole life as a missionary all over the world and then he dies here in Spain of a heart attack while visiting his sisters.
ANA: Your first love. . .
LAURA: Don't be silly. It was puppy love!
ANA: I bet you would have married him!
LAURA: Well, that's fate for you!
ANA: Fate? It was those priests at his school, the collection plates for the missionaries, the apostle saving the pagans. . . They were probably better off without it. There are always things that get in the way. You can't blame everything on fate. Hey, is this the same upholstery?
LAURA: The same, just older.
ANA: I could have sworn it was lighter. . . brighter. The truth is everything looks very different to me. Everything is smaller, more depressing. . . even the window. It was always so hard to get open and just now I opened it and it wasn't hard at all.
LAURA: Mother had the windows planed down; they didn't shut right.
ANA: Oh! For a moment there I thought distance had made me lose all notion of perspective. It could be that the room looks smaller with all these boxes in the way. *(Walks toward the window.)* The street certainly has changed. . . the traffic. . . *(Looking.)* Even the porticos. General Franco's portrait isn't there anymore. . . I always thought it was indelible.
LAURA *(Coming closer)*: So many things have changed. I think for the worse. Look! There! Do you see that orange neon sign?
ANA: "Video-Sex"! In this town? But, isn't that. . .?
LAURA: Yes, it sure is. Mrs. Garcia's stationery store. When she died her sons moved the store and well, now. . .

ANA: Do you remember that woman? With those hairdos of hers? How tacky! She used to sell us that blue paper to cover our books...
LAURA: And the packages of sky blue wrapping paper we used at Christmas.
ANA: And onion skin to trace embroidery patterns...
LAURA: And construction paper to make flowers for the Virgin...
ANA: I'd say that except for toilet paper she kept us pretty well supplied. We must have bought tons of paper from her... and look where it's gotten us!
LAURA: What do you mean?
ANA: Don't you see it? We spent twelve years in school! Twelve useless years in school filling up notebook after notebook with the same sentences until we produced graceful script penmanship. We put covers on hundreds of books that didn't say anything real! And flowers for the Virgin? How many flowers did we make in twelve years? And tracing? Afternoons spent tracing patterns of flowers to put on embroidery. With the wonderful sewing machines they have nowadays!
LAURA: Technology! Who would have ever guessed you'd be able to solve your entire hope chest problem by pressing four little buttons.
ANA: To hell with technology! It's the piece of crap education they gave us!
LAURA: It doesn't seem like it... you swear so naturally you'd think you came right out of one of today's classrooms.
ANA: I'd love to... start over!
LAURA: Well, now that we're swearing, I'll let you know that I liked the damned flowers and the embroidering. They had their charm. What I couldn't stand were all the prayers. Morning prayer, afternoon prayers, novenas for every lousy thing that ever happened and those endless rosaries. Did you ever notice what horrible knees all of us who went to Catholic school have? They're awful. I ended up getting sick and tired of mass. And you know what? I haven't been to mass in ages. Thank God no one notices that kind of thing in Madrid. The only problem is when I go to confession...
ANA *(Laughing)*: You haven't changed a bit. You're the same person you were twenty years ago. I thought you would have changed. I've changed so much.
LAURA: You think so? I think people never change. Nothing can ever make us change. Mother never changed. Antonio is the same person who sat next to me at the old movie house. Dad was different for a few days right after you left, but he was soon back to his old self. No one changes. You, yourself, said you've changed and yet I see the same old you... frightened... elusive... the same old Ana I've always known. You just admitted it yourself when you were talking about Father's portrait.

ANA: Now there's something that doesn't change. . . the dead. They're trapped. In portraits. . . in different things. . . with that same old look. *(She approaches the portrait.)* Did he suffer a lot when he died?
LAURA: Yes. He spent nights screaming. The tranquilizers didn't work. There were eleven horrible nights. . . Mother and I. . . taking turns. . . hoping it would be over soon. We were alone. . .
ANA: I'm sorry. It was impossible for me to come. We had just gotten settled in Paris. We had no money. . . I . . .
LAURA: Don't apologize. I understand. What really upset me was you not coming when Mother died. . . at least the funeral. It was really beautiful. She would have liked. . .
ANA: Don't be ridiculous, Laura!
LAURA: I'm not being ridiculous! Mother always wanted her life and her funeral to be dignified. While she was alive, I did what I could, and when she died, I did what she wanted, and I'm proud of it. The only bad part was that, once again, I had to do it by myself. I needed you. . . you should have come.
ANA: I couldn't. Please forgive me. I know it's very difficult for me to justify myself, but after Mother and I hadn't seen each other for such a long time. After everything with Father, coming for her funeral seemed like a farce. Besides, everything happened so suddenly. . .
LAURA: Come on, Ana. Don't disguise it. Coming then seemed like a farce, but yet you were able to come today.
ANA: It's different. They're not here anymore.
LAURA: You just said that doesn't change things, that they're still trapped in objects. Be honest. We know each other too well. You're petrified of the dead. We slept in the same room for years. I've heard you cry and remember you coming to my bed shaking. You would always dream about dead people, and I'm sure the same dreams still haunt you. You didn't care what I felt. You didn't come because this time the dead person was your mother and it scared you beyond belief. . . and you made excuses to me, an endless series of stupid excuses just like when we were little and you would say you had a stomach ache.
ANA: You haven't forgiven me.
LAURA: Of course I've forgiven you. . . because I understand you. It's easy to forgive when you understand things. But I was very lonely. . . I was the one who needed you.
ANA: You had Antonio, the kids. . .
LAURA: It's different. I needed you. They're part of another family. I don't know how to explain it. They're my second family. It's the other family, your first family, that you're closer to and the one that you really need.

Your first family is the one that teaches you how to understand the second one. Anyway, it had been so long since you left us, that I already had practice. That made it easier, but I thought. . . well, who cares what I thought. It's water under the bridge, like Dad used to say.
ANA: Like all his sayings, he was wrong. Water under the bridge? It depends how bad the flood is.
LAURA *(Taking the packages)*: How about something to eat? I brought a bunch of things.
ANA: The truth is I'm not that hungry.
LAURA: Well, the pastries are delicious and so are the sandwiches. You can start unpacking them. Look, we have wine, too.
ANA: And good wine at that!
LAURA: The occasion calls for it.
ANA *(Looking at the wrapping paper on the food)*: The Little Princess Bakery! It's still around?
LAURA: Yes, and now they have a take out and a café.
ANA: The eclairs were so good there!
LAURA: And the macaroons! When Mother was still alive we would come here on weekends and take carloads of them back with us.
ANA: I loved them!
LAURA: But they don't make them like they used to. They're not as sweet and they're smaller. Nothing is like it used to be anymore.
ANA: No. Where are the wine glasses?
LAURA: Hold on. Probably in the kitchen. *(Exits.)*
ANA: Bring a corkscrew!
LAURA *(Offstage)*: That might not be so easy!

(ANA walks around the room, looking for a place to put the food down and trips over her sister's coat. She goes to put it away somewhere else and starts feeling it. She puts the coat over her shoulders to see how it looks on her. LAURA appears behind her, with some wine glasses and a corkscrew, and watches her in silence.)

LAURA: It looks wonderful on you!
ANA *(Somewhat embarrassed, quickly takes off the coat and puts it on a chair)*: Sorry, I was just curious. I've never worn fur. I don't think it looks good on me, and that's lucky since it's so expensive.
LAURA: Well, I think it looks wonderful on you. Looks like it was custom made. It was an anniversary present from Antonio. Here are the wine glasses and the corkscrew.
ANA: Mother's glassware. . . There are still pieces left?

Packing up the Past-15

LAURA: Yes, these two. *(Opens the bottle.)* Here, help yourself.
ANA: How many years have you been married?
LAURA: Twenty! Forever! Try the sandwiches, you'll see how good they are. *(After a pause to let her finish chewing.)* Look, I hope it's okay with you but I gave all of Mother's clothes except for a few very old things to the nuns.
ANA: Our nuns?
LAURA: Yes, they're in charge of distributing clothes to the poor. I figured you wouldn't be interested in them. . . most were somber mourning clothes.
ANA: I think it's a great idea. Do you want some wine?
LAURA: Yes, please. It'll help us warm up. Since we had the electricity turned off, we can't turn on the heat.
ANA: Why did you have it turned off?
LAURA: It was Antonio's idea. He thinks it's silly to keep paying if we don't come by here anymore.
ANA: Don't you still come on weekends?
LAURA: No. Mother was the only reason we came. She enjoyed seeing the kids.
ANA: Why didn't you take her to Madrid with you?
LAURA: And make her leave her home? Forget it. She didn't want to leave this place. Her friends, her memories. . . they were all here. It would have been cruel to make her leave.
ANA: And what about the school? Our school? Do they still use it? Since you were talking about the poor. . .
LAURA: Yes, of course it's still in operation. Helping the poor is something extra the nuns do. Now the girls wear different uniforms, and I think the nuns aren't as strict.
ANA: Thank God! Our uniforms were so ugly. Remember those berets?
LAURA: I liked them, they were cute.
ANA: Because they looked good on you, but I looked awful. What I don't understand is why you came back so often to visit after you were married. You hated this town as much as I did.
LAURA: At first we came because of Dad, then because of Mother. . . and because of Antonio's family, too. The truth is I've led a very family oriented life. I'd spend all week home by myself, the kids at school, Antonio at work and when Saturday finally came, we'd all get in the car and drive to our hometown to take care of the rest of the family. And if you promise not to laugh, I'll tell you something else. . .
ANA: What?
LAURA: I couldn't wait for Saturday to come. Coming to this little town has been my only distraction for years. Can you believe it? Spend my whole life dreaming about being a cosmopolitan Bette Davis type and I turn into a

country bumpkin who hates Madrid. Deep down inside I must really be a hick.

ANA: I was the one who wanted to be Bette Davis, remember? You wanted to be Mrs. Miniver.

LAURA: You're right. Speaking of which, I have to call Mrs. Miniver's sweet home. When she's not there, everything is a mess. *(She goes to the phone and dials. Her sister finishes eating and listens to the conversation)* Emilia? It's Mrs. Castillo. Are the children home yet? Mr. Castillo? No, there's no need for you to make dinner. If he doesn't come for lunch, he probably won't be home for dinner. If my son comes, cook him some fish. . . make sure it's not too well done. . . What? And he didn't tell you why he wouldn't be home for dinner? Well, just save it for tomorrow night then. If my daughter is late, just start without her. You know how she is, always forgetting to call. I'm still here. No, I won't be home tonight either. Tell them to call me here. Thank you, Emilia. See you tomorrow. *(She hangs up, walks towards the table, and pours herself another glass of wine.)*

ANA: You'd think it was a stampede. . .

LAURA: It's always like that, and the worst part is they don't even bother calling. I don't mind so much for myself. I'm used to it. But they could be a little more considerate with the help, especially with good help so hard to find. But tonight they're going to hear it, especially the boy. . .

ANA: He's not that much of a boy anymore. After all, he's seventeen. I picture him just like his father, with Antonio's frizzy hair.

LAURA: Hair? He wears it so short, he barely has any. . . and he has an earring. Well, he really just has his ear pierced, because Antonio would kill him if he actually catches him wearing one. And he has a face full of pimples. Just like his father did. He's crazy and I don't understand him, but he's not a bad kid. He's a pacifist, an environmentalist, a mountain climber, a conscientious objector, a nudist. In short, part of every new fad. Although fortunately, he hasn't gotten into politics or drugs. You have to come over sometime soon, now that we've broken the ice.

ANA: What ice?

LAURA: Well, I mean now that you're around here again. . . that we've had a chance to see each other. Besides, there's no excuse now that we both live in Madrid.

ANA: You're right. . . now that we've broken the ice. *(She gets up and observes a painting on the floor.)* What are you planning to do with this painting?

LAURA: Me? Nothing. Except for Father's portrait and two or three other pieces, the rest are hideous.

ANA: Do you want Father's portrait?

LAURA: Unless you object. . . I always liked it.

ANA: Be my guest. . . you can have it. I like this one better.
LAURA *(Does so)*: I don't see anything.
LAURA *(Coming closer)*: This one? It's nothing special. . . just some shepherds.
ANA: I always thought it was comical. Do you remember? It was right in front of Father's desk in his office and he never noticed. . . Look!
LAURA *(Does so)*: I don't see anything.
ANA: You don't see it there? In the background! In the pasture in the back. . . the bull mounting the cow!
LAURA: They're? *(Laughing.)* No! Dad couldn't have noticed. . . otherwise he would've never allowed it.
ANA: Father. . . so strict, so upright, so moral. . . and he was blind to what was going on right in front of his face. He never noticed little things.
LAURA: Like us. . .
ANA: What did you say?
LAURA: Nothing, just being silly.
ANA: No, you said something that made a lot of sense. I always thought it was my own obsession, but now I see that you saw it too.
LAURA: Saw what?
ANA: He never noticed us. We were in the house just like any other object. He never took the time to talk to us, to get to know us. We were just two more of a number of household decorations. He gave us the same superficial treatment he gave other little things. The same way he looked at this painting. . . without even noticing what was really going on.
LAURA: Well, so little was really going on with us anyway.
ANA: That's true. Do you know when I remembered this scene and understood what it meant? When I first arrived in Chile I spent a summer at a ranch and I saw two horses mating. Suddenly, this scene came to mind. I had always thought it was such a silly idea. . . two big animals playing games like that. I felt like such an idiot for it to take so many years to see such a beautiful moment, especially when we lived in a small town and farms and animals were only a mile away. It would've been so great to see that as a child. . . with Dad there to explain what was going on. You have no idea how ridiculous you feel when you're a grown woman and you've been sleeping with a man you're not married to and you see the face he makes when you ask him what the horses are doing. . .
LAURA: Believe me, I understand. If it wasn't for the fact that I'm too embarrassed, I'd tell you about my wedding night. But, hey. . .even after all these years I'm still too embarrassed to tell you.
ANA: Same here. . . you should have seen my first time!

Amparo Rivelles and Lola Cardona in 1985 production at Real Coliseo de Carlos III. Photo by Manuel Martínez Muñoz.

LAURA: Oh boy! You have to tell me about that one! I've spent many a night wondering what it was like. And in your first letter after two months you didn't breathe a word about it! It drove me nuts! So this time you're not getting away without telling me about it. Wait a minute... I'm getting myself a shot of cognac. *(She does so.)* Would you like some?

ANA: No, the wine's enough for me. I'm not used to drinking.

LAURA: I never used to drink either, but lately I've realized what an idiot I've been. A little drink now and then doesn't hurt anyone...

ANA: Well, you'll have to pour me another drink to get me to talk...

LAURA: Of course you'll talk. At least I'll get to find out... even if it's after all these years. *(She pours her a drink and sits down next to ANA, who lights a cigarette.)*

ANA: I don't drink, but I'm a chain smoker...

LAURA: I don't enjoy smoking at all. Come on, though! Tell me about what it was like with Juan...

ANA: It really wasn't a big deal...

LAURA: How can you say that? I still remember when he would pick you up by the portico on Sundays. I spied on you so many times! You would walk down Main Street, he would follow you, at a cautious distance. By the time you reached the church, he would be right behind you. I could see how he would get closer and closer to you, but then I would have to turn back because you could see anyone who followed you beyond that point... and I would go back home thinking about him kissing and hugging you...

ANA: Well, until the day we ran off together, we had never even kissed.

LAURA: I can't believe that! You should have told me earlier. You have no idea the scenes my overactive imagination created. The first night, when you ran off... you wouldn't believe what I pictured. The two of you fleeing in a sleeper car with a bottle of champagne, the rocking back and forth of the train... I was so jealous! Did he have a hairy chest?

ANA: What does that have to do with anything?

LAURA: Answer me! He was very hairy, right?

ANA: Yes.

LAURA: I thought so. Very dark?

ANA: Dark? No, I don't think so... I don't remember.

LAURA: How could you forget something like that? You're not supposed to forget those kinds of things.

ANA: Well, if it's any consolation to you, I'll have you know that you probably had a better time than I did that night because there was no sleeper car, no champagne, and no rocking back and forth of the train. We spent our first night in a cheap little hotel in some hick town waiting for a connecting

train. And we were so tired and it was so cold that I didn't get the chance to see the hair on his chest for the next two days. He wore an undershirt.
LAURA: An undershirt? Like Father? What a disappointment! Must've have been a horrible night.
ANA: Can you imagine? The cold... I was so inexperienced... and with that stranger on top of me. The only thing I remember was that the bed made a lot of noise and I kept thinking about the neighbors, who I could hear snoring next door... and that man on top of me the whole time. It took forever...
LAURA: It was the exact opposite for me. The whole thing was over in no time.
ANA: Really? You mean Antonio... *(Laughs.)*
LAURA: See, now you're making me talk. No, not always. I think he was just as much of a virgin as I was. He was very nervous... and *(She laughs.)* Anyway, neither one of us knew which way was up. *(Both laugh.)*
ANA: There's nothing worse than feeling ridiculous at times like that.
LAURA: Why did you and Juan break up?
ANA: Who knows? It's easy to know how things start, but you really never quite know what ends a relationship. Maybe I was too young. So many things changed so quickly that it was probably too much for me to handle all at once. I don't know...
LAURA: Did he leave you in the lurch?
ANA: I was the one who left him.
LAURA: You left him? You were brave enough?
ANA: Well, not exactly brave. You see, around that time I met someone else...
LAURA: Carlos?
ANA: No, Carlos came much later.
LAURA: But you... How many men have you been with?
ANA: Several...
LAURA: Several! You say it so matter-of-factly... tell me about them!
ANA: No way! You've already gotten me to tell you too much. It's so hard for me to talk about myself. Besides, we have to hurry. I have to catch the last train, unless I want to lose my job... It took me so long to find one.
LAURA: Fine, we'll keep working, but you always whet my appetite. You used to do the same to me when we were little. You just loved to keep me guessing. I'd give anything to know what you've been up to these last few years.
ANA: We'll get to see each other more now that I'm living in Madrid. There'll be plenty of time for you to find out more. What else can I help with?
LAURA: Let's start sealing some of the boxes and moving them towards the door. That way we'll know which ones are full.

ANA: Whatever you say as long as I don't have to go upstairs to the bedroom. The stairway always made me dizzy.
LAURA: You were always such a mess when we were kids. . . afraid of this, dizzy from that, one complex after another.
ANA: To tell you the truth I haven't changed that much.
LAURA: We should have tossed you in the garbage when you were born. I wasn't that off target when I was little and insisted on trading you in. I wanted a boy so whenever we went to the fabric shop I tried to get Mother to exchange you for something else.
ANA: At the fabric store?
LAURA: Of course. Mother spent her life exchanging things there. I think she must have set a world's record for trips back and forth to the fabric shop.
ANA: She was always very insecure. The whole situation with me must have affected her deeply.
LAURA: Especially because of Father's attitude. She never mentioned you while he was alive. She knew there was no solution and that you would never come back unless he forgave you. But she had a hard time with it when he died and you didn't come around, although she never said anything. You remember how she was. . .
ANA: No, she never said anything. She was content to never say anything, never bother anyone. She always had the same attitude: a hateful silence. How could our mother never have anything to say to us in her own right? All of her warnings, advice, and little talks revolved around Father's instructions. I wonder if she ever had a single idea of her own. . .
LAURA: I don't think so. She probably had the same problem with ideas that she had at the fabric shop. . . she couldn't make up her mind. She always had to rely on someone else's judgment. I understand her. . . I'm like her in so many ways. . . Poor thing!
ANA: What's in these boxes? They weigh a ton.
LAURA: China in that one. And I think pots and pans in this one. Mother always had a good supply of those. Maybe they'll come in handy now that you're setting up your home.
ANA: No. I refuse to set up a home and do the kitchen all at once. I hate the range and avoid cooking whenever I can.
LAURA: But you loved the kitchen as a child.
ANA: I loved the kitchen because it was the warmest place in the house. And besides Ramona was always there telling us stories about ghosts and witches. At bedtime I'd be scared to death.
LAURA: They never scared me. What used to scare me was Aunt Susana. Remember her? Remember how she would watch over the length of our

skirts? She never thought they were long enough. Hems were a measure of morality to her.

ANA: She always wore her hems down to her ankles.

LAURA: Because she had varicose veins! When she died I helped Mother shroud her. It was the first time I had ever seen her legs and they were horrible.

ANA: You've spent your whole life taking care of the dead.

LAURA: You know how it is in Spain. Women spend their whole lives taking care of someone: first it's their dolls, then their children, their husbands, the dead, saints, other women, the poor. . . It's our curse. After all, we used to like playing house. That's why I don't make Yoli do any housework. Not that it takes much to get her to avoid it.

ANA: Well, this is the last box. Are there any more?

LAURA: In the kitchen and the sitting room, but they're already sealed. Do you sleep in a double bed?

ANA: Why do you ask?

LAURA: Because Antonio and I sleep in separate beds since he gets up so early and I'm an insomniac. Mother had a number of brand new sheet sets she never even used. If you have a double bed you could get some use out of them.

ANA: That's not a bad idea. The truth is I could really use them.

LAURA: Well then, I'll get them right now and we can wrap them up for you. I think there's some paper and string over in that corner.

ANA *(Takes out a cigarette and lights it, goes to take a sip of cognac, and suddenly turns towards her father's portrait and makes a toast)*: To you, Dad! *(She drinks and then goes to look for the paper and string. The pieces of the picture she ripped up earlier are on the sofa. She looks at them, picks them up, and puts them in her pocket.)*

LAURA *(Appears with a pile of bed linens)*: Help! I can't believe how much this weighs! Especially, since they're linen. Look at this embroidery! It's handmade! Plus, they're brand new.

ANA: The bad part about linen is ironing it.

LAURA: Well, I even make them iron permanent press. I love sleeping on freshly ironed sheets.

ANA: Me too, but I don't like having to iron them myself. Do you remember our bedspreads?

LAURA: They were such a pain! They had to be washed, starched, ironed. . . but they looked great. Too bad we weren't allowed to sit on them. Mother used to get so angry. . .

ANA: Everything in that house was just for looks. . . including our brains. Everything was there for decoration and so that company could enjoy it.

Packing up the Past-23

We couldn't lie on our bedspreads or go to bed without properly hanging up our clothes.
LAURA: And we weren't allowed to leave the house if we didn't make our beds.
ANA: That's right. I'm such an idiot I've even made the bed in hotel rooms. And nobody but us could wash our underwear...
LAURA: And we only went into the parlor and the sitting room when we had company. They were the forbidden zones. At times I even forgot they were part of the same house.
ANA: We were always restricted to that hateful family room. We could never step on the hardwood floor... Strictly against the rules!
LAURA: We were only allowed on the wood to wax it...
ANA: And we weren't allowed to press our faces up against the windows because they would streak. Do you know how many times I got in trouble for drawing pictures on foggy windows?
LAURA: And we'd get in trouble for locking ourselves in the bathroom...
ANA: Or in the bedroom...
LAURA: And they would open our letters before they gave them to us...
ANA: We weren't allowed to go out with the Rodriguez girls either...
LAURA: Because their father was a communist...
ANA: But they always went out with the cutest boys in town...
LAURA: Well, of course... they allowed themselves to be kissed!
ANA: And the record player! We weren't allowed to use it during Holy Week.
LAURA: And makeup? I never wore makeup in front of Father until I was twenty! Smoke? I could never do it in front if him!
ANA: Yet he always had that cloud of smoke around him from his cigars...
LAURA: He wouldn't let us go out with boys...
ANA: And we weren't allowed to talk on the phone. The phone is for important conversations! Our chit chats and gossiping on the phone were never important...
LAURA: And we had to be home by nine o'clock... No excuses!
ANA: All buttons buttoned to the top! On Sundays we had to wear our veils all morning...
LAURA: Children don't speak to adults! Children only answer when spoken to.
ANA: We came out ahead on that one. If we asked, they only lied to us anyway...
LAURA: Everything was forbidden: talking to strangers, talking too loud, sometimes talking too softly for that matter, laughing, jumping in the house, dancing.
ANA: At least we were allowed to cry, only not in front of them...

24- Sebastián Junyent

LAURA: Comic books were inappropriate...
ANA: Just like medical school!
LAURA: Marriage is a woman's career!
ANA: This house was worse than a concentration camp! And then besides they had the nerve to tell us all those prohibitions were for our own good!
LAURA: I obeyed... I got married.
ANA: In the end, I did too. And I didn't go to medical school.
LAURA: Your big dream. Remember when we'd take naps in the summer? We'd watch the shadows on the ceiling... reflections of the sun coming through the blinds...
ANA: When the leaves on the trees shook they would form pictures on the ceiling. Sometimes they took on human shapes... It was like the movies. We'd let our imaginations run wild and make those reflections part of movies we starred in. I operated on appendixes and won the Nobel Prize for my research...
LAURA: And I would walk into the chapel, wearing a dress with a long train. It's funny... I don't remember what the groom's face looked like, but the man giving me away was always Spencer Tracy... Father Tracy...
ANA: Do you know how many times we saw *Father of the Bride*? We used to love going to the movies! Running all the way to the church, praying to Saint Nicholas...
LAURA: Saint Nicholas, patron saint of the impossible. Please don't make the movie Rated G and I'll say you a whole rosary!
ANA: But it never worked! They were almost always insipid movies suitable for children... except for *Singing in the Rain*. I must have seen that movie a million times... I still remember the music to it... *(Starts humming.)*
LAURA: You're right! So do I! *(She hums also. It would then be great for both actresses to sing a bit off tune and dance around to some song.)*
ANA: Singing is definitely not our thing. *(She sits.)*
LAURA *(Serving herself more cognac)*: Our singing is perfect. Would you like some more? *(ANA shakes her head no.)* It's too bad we spent years taking useless sewing lessons instead of voice lessons.
ANA: They lied to us even in that. We would have forgotten all the music we learned anyway, just like we forgot how to sew... at least I did.
LAURA: Goodness gracious, so did I! Boy, can I feel the years! *(Sits down across from her. Pause.)* Well, almost everything is done. Let's sit and rest a while and unless you object, we should get down to talking about less pleasant things.
ANA *(Lighting another cigarette)*: Haven't we spoken about enough things that are unpleasant?

LAURA: I'm referring to financial matters. There are several things we have to discuss.

ANA: You tell me.

LAURA *(She gets up and looks for a folder, sits down again and opens it)*: Well, we have to decide what we want to do with the house. Then there are stocks, valuables, jewelry. As you can see, there are a number of items.

ANA *(Making herself comfortable)*: Start wherever you want.

LAURA: Well, we may as well start with Mother's jewelry. Here's the list. The jewelry is in a safe deposit box at the bank. As you see, each piece is described and grouped in a lot according to its value. We had everything appraised by a reputable jeweler. . . the same one Mother always used. *(She gives ANA the list.)*

ANA: I didn't know mother had a jeweler. I thought she only had a handful of costume jewelry.

LAURA: Not quite. Dad bought her a lot of jewelry toward the end, some of it very expensive. Look at the value.

ANA: My God! She must have looked like a statue of the Virgin Mary decked out for Holy Week!

LAURA: Actually, she barely wore any. She was afraid she would lose it. I think there are some things she never even wore once. Look. As you can see, we're talking about too much money not to discuss it with you. Antonio has. . .well, we have tried to find a way to solve the dividing up problem in a logical way which is fair to both of us. I'm sure the terms will be satisfactory to you.

ANA: Satisfactory? I don't think I understand.

LAURA: We were thinking that since you have no children, you would be willing to give your share of the jewelry to Yoli. As the only granddaughter. We think it's most logical for her to have them to pass on. We would, of course, compensate you monetarily for your share. Antonio thinks that after the house is sold, you could take your half plus another third as compensation for the jewelry. I hope you find that agreeable. We've appraised the value of the house and how much we could probably get for it. If you take half that plus the third for the jewelry and your share of the stocks and valuables, you'll see it's a pretty hefty sum. I'm sure it would come in handy, now that you're getting settled in Madrid. To me, at least. . . the truth is I think it's a good deal.

ANA *(Slowly reads the list, then looks straight at her sister)*: In other words, you and your husband think that it's a good idea for me to give my half of the jewelry to your daughter since she's the only granddaughter. And since I'll be very well compensated for them financially, you think I should be satisfied. . . Is that it?

LAURA: I think it's an excellent offer!
ANA: You're so sure I'll accept. . . since I need the money. And since I have no children, my niece should inherit all of her beloved grandmother's jewels. And what makes you so sure Aunt Ana has no children?
LAURA: Do you?
ANA: What a mystery! After having been around all over, I could've very well brought a child into this world. . . Don't you think?
LAURA: I think you're pulling my leg. You would have told me by now if you had a child.
ANA: Are you sure? You just found out a minute ago that I was married. Why wouldn't you find out now that you're an aunt. You know how full of surprises I can be. . .
LAURA: I don't know. I'm sure you would've told me. You wouldn't hide something like that from me. You shouldn't joke about something so serious. Come on, stop kidding around. Do you or don't you have a child?
ANA: Well, it's about time! At least you admit I could have had one. *(Pause.)* I'm starting to understand your. . . or should I say your and Antonio's urgency for me to come to the house. Everything is already underway. All ready for a smooth transfer of ownership. But there's one small detail left to be taken care of: the jewelry. And since selling the house is so complicated, you and Antonio, in a particularly lucid moment, set up this scenario. . . a trip down memory lane with the excuse of picking up a couple of pictures. And then you con me into signing away in compliance to your wishes. James Cagney and Bette Davis couldn't have done a better job.
LAURA: You're wrong. This isn't some kind of scheme. I needed to see you. It wasn't a matter of taking care of the house or the jewelry. You would have let me handle everything. All I had to do was liquidate and mail you your half of the money. That would've been good enough for you. If I made you come today. . . It's because. . . it's because I needed to see you. It's important that we spend the last minutes in this house together. That was my only intention. I swear to you.
ANA: You don't have to swear to me. I'm sure that was your intention. But what about your husband's intentions? He's much more practical than you are. He probably figured it was a good way to kill two birds with one stone.
LAURA: Don't be silly. It's as if you were insinuating that Antonio and I are trying to cheat you out of something. The house has to be sold. When I spoke to you about it you agreed. The jewelry is there. You didn't even know most of it existed. If we were trying to cheat you, we wouldn't have even called you.
ANA: I would have found out through the will.

LAURA: I think it's ridiculous for us to continue this conversation. I'm sure you agree that my daughter has her rights as the only granddaughter.
ANA: The only recognized one.
LAURA: Would you please stop kidding around? If it's true that you're a mother, say so once and for all and be done with it!
ANA: Would you change your plans if it were true? Would things be divided up differently?
LAURA: You decide. It's your right. According to the will, you have every right. . .
ANA: And according to you. . . do I have the right?
LAURA: I think you could care less about what I think. You've always done whatever you wanted.
ANA: Of course I have. But you haven't answered my question. Answer me: Do I have the right?
LAURA: Do you want me to be honest?
ANA: I'd like you to be.
LAURA: I don't think you have a right to anything. When you took off, you didn't give a damn about what you left behind. When times were hard, when I needed you the most, you always got out of it. There were always ample excuses: being too far away, no money, a new love, fear. . . Anything except coming to deal with it, like I did. Tell me, what gives you the right to come here now? There have been more auspicious occasions. . . at least times when it would have been more dignified. Yet now that there's the possibility of getting some money out of it, you come around with your clean little hands to pick it up. And I'm against it. . . Do you hear me? Against it! But I don't let it bother me because I have no choice. So you get some money out of it. But Mother's jewelry. . . Everything else. . . I won't let you have it. It's mine because I earned it. . . Earned it for putting up with our father after you left. Because when you left, you condemned me to them for the rest of my life. I was the only idiot who stuck around here to console them. If I had followed in your footsteps. . . I've put up with everything. I didn't have the chance to choose a boyfriend. I married the boy next door. After all, no one better came around. I've put up with sickness, death. . . I'm the one who saw them die. And you have no idea how slowly a parent can die. I've always been the good sister, the one who did everything she was supposed to. . . the idiot. And to top it all off, our dear mother, who never had an opinion about anything, decides in her magnanimous last hour that you should inherit half of everything. Don't you think it's just too ironic? So I have to take it, because I'm not about to fight over four lousy rooms. They're not worth it. . . but at least allow me the right to kick and scream.

28- Sebastián Junyent

ANA: It's about time! You've finally let out all the bile in your system. That's how our conversation today should have started. If you had told me all this when I first got here, we'd both feel better now. But no. . . you just said it yourself. You've spent the whole afternoon being the "good" sister. . . so understanding. You've sugarcoated everything for me. . . surrounded me with all this emotional bullshit and just when all my defenses were down. . . Bam! You hit me up with your little plan. That's manipulation!

LAURA: That's a lie. None of this was premeditated. Too many years have gone by to be reproachful. If I have been, it's so you understand that I'm the one who feels used. That this whole will is unfair. That it hasn't been worth it for me to sacrifice my whole life. That's the only thing I care about, and that's why I just said what I said. And if I made you come today, and if I've been pleasant and sweet to you, it's because I needed you, like I've needed you before and because I knew that this time you would come because you need the money. It's the only chance I've had to be with you. You're the one who asked me to take care of everything. Just think how easy it would've been for me to wrap it all up and send you a check. Don't you realize that I need you? I have the right to be scared sometimes too.

ANA: I'm sorry. It's just that it bothers me when people try to plan out my life. When you told me about your plan. . . about the jewelry. . . I felt like I had no say. And it hurt. Maybe because it's the truth. But after being here together, after all this talk about our lives. . . I thought I had a say in this house. Until you read me the game rules. I have no right to profane anything. Mother's heirlooms should stay in the family. Suddenly you've restored me to my place as an outsider. I. . . Well, you know I. . . I wasn't planning to come today. I was embarrassed to come for something that, like you said, doesn't belong to me. If it were up to me, I wouldn't have come. I wouldn't have even asked you for any part of it. But I'm not alone. . . There's Carlos. . . I need the money. . . He suggested that I come, because men, you see, have evolved. They no longer demand, they suggest. He can't understand that I would have any qualms about collecting this inheritance. He doesn't care. When it comes down to it, I'm the one who has to face the music. . . And the money is well worth facing it for. And so I come, and I face the music, because I have no choice. Because I need the money to survive. And because I don't want to argue with him, don't want him to be angry with me. . . Because I'm afraid. . . Afraid of losing him. . . Afraid of being alone. That's why I'm here. . . with no right. My only right was to the conversation we just had. Now I have no other right left.

LAURA *(Pouring her another drink)*: Here, drink this. I think we've both overreacted. If we need a solution, we'll find one. But tell me, have you had any children?

ANA: No. Just a miscarriage. I was only a few months pregnant. That's it, nothing else.
LAURA: I'm sorry. You may be right about what you said. We were getting along so well. . . Then Antonio's damned list had to ruin it.
ANA: See that? Antonio's list. Here we are, lashing into each other like fools, in order to protect the financial interests of our husbands. We'll never change. Decisions are always being made for us, and all we do is obey.
LAURA: Antonio is different. He does it for me. He doesn't care about the money. He's willing to keep the house and give you your half of the money. He wants me to keep the house if I want. He knows how much it means to me.
ANA: What? He's planning to buy the house so you can use it?
LAURA: Yes. As soon as you sign the papers, he's willing to remodel. He wants us to be able to come on weekends. He knows how much I love this little town.
ANA: When did he decide this?
LAURA: From the start. That's why he wanted to make sure we took care of the situation with the house as soon as possible.
ANA: You're kidding me? Then why did you put it up for sale?
LAURA: We haven't put it up for sale,.
ANA *(She quickly gets up and looks for a newspaper clipping in her pocketbook and shows it to her sister)*: Then what about this ad? It's been there for days. This is the address. And it describes the house, although the asking price is higher than the appraised value. *(Signals the list.)*
LAURA *(Shocked)*: I can't believe it. He. . . He couldn't have. It's his office phone number. . . Why did he do it? He always said. . . This house is mine! He has no right! Without asking me, he has no right!
ANA: It seems that he. . .
LAURA: There must be some kind of mistake. . .
ANA: My God, Laura! Stop ignoring what you don't want to see. People don't make a mistake like putting an ad in the paper for ten days. And what about the lights? You told me he had them turned off. Why? If you planned on using the house, it makes no sense.
LAURA: The utilities. . . Of course. . . But. . . Why hasn't he had the phone turned off? He could have done that too.
ANA: You can always get more money for a place with phone service. If you read the ad, it advertises it as an amenity.
LAURA *(Reading)*: Two floors, twelve rooms, two bathrooms, telephone. That's ridiculous. He knows he can't sell anything if I don't agree to it. I have to give my permission.

Packing up the Past, directed by Martín Ferrer and starring Mara Goyanes and Conchita Goyanes. Real Coliseo de Carlos III, El Escorial, December 1993. Photo by Manuel Martínez Muñoz.

ANA: I don't think he's too worried. I'm sure he'll find a way to convince you once he's found a buyer.
LAURA: Now that you mention it, he said something that I didn't pay much attention to. . . something about problems with taxes, but. . .Why did he lie to me?
ANA: Money. From what you just said, Antonio is the perfect businessman. You could tell ever since he was a kid. Remember when he used to rent us his Monopoly game?
LAURA: How could he sink so low? He thinks I'm a puppet he can manipulate.
ANA: Don't kid yourself. He hasn't given it a second thought. You and I are both puppets that let anyone control us. Think about it. It's our own fault.
LAURA: No, I don't want to think. It's better not to think. What for? To realize that I have no ideas of my own? It's not even worth thinking. As you can see, everyone else does my thinking for me.
ANA: But it shouldn't be that way. We should be the ones to think. We're the only ones responsible for our own lives. Enough of taking the easy way out. Always blaming everyone else. The only thing they do is take advantage of the opportunities we give them. We shouldn't let down our guard. We have to think for ourselves and not let them manipulate us anymore. I'm sick of it. I've spent my life as a suitcase. Just like a suitcase, I've let them take me wherever they wanted. Sometimes they've treated me gently, like you would treat a fine leather suitcase. Other times I've been shuffled around more roughly than cheap second hand luggage. They've packed and unpacked whatever the hell they wanted inside me. They've stamped me, labeled me, kicked me around. At best checked me through to a destination. All too often I've been left at the baggage check. And there I sat, ready, waiting for them to come fetch me. And when they search you, that's the worst. The value they put on you when they can't find what they were looking for after they've done. Then you sit there, with your insides scattered about waiting for someone else to come by and put everything back together again. We're suitcases, Laura. We don't even get to be trunks. At least they have a hard exterior and protective metal strips. They can be arrogant, because they can't be violated. We're just suitcases.
LAURA: I must be an empty suitcase.
ANA: Someone will always come around to fill you with his things. He'll utilize every available little corner for his belongings. And if he's smart, he'll try not to overstuff you so you won't break open. And if you start to split, he'll tie you with a cord. Especially if the leather still looks good. *(She touches LAURA's cheek, who slowly moves away and serves herself more cognac.)*
LAURA *(Drinks)*: I've heard that alcohol gets rid of skin spots. . .

ANA: If and when you don't drown them in it.
LAURA: It's true. I think that the suitcase analogy is applicable to all of us. Mother was like the suitcases the soldiers used to use. . . those small, striped, hard ones. They lasted forever but were easily neglected. What about Aunt Susana? What kind of a suitcase do you think she was?
ANA: She wasn't a suitcase. She was a duffle bag.
LAURA: Yolanda is a duffle bag too. . . a duffle bag with a bunch of holes, that everything falls out of. You know there's something in there, but when you go to get it, you can't find it. It's gone.
ANA *(Pours herself a drink)*: What do you feel when you have a child?
LAURA: Fear! And then you feel a great calm, but it doesn't last. Fear quickly returns and then it never goes away. You're afraid of sicknesses, accidents, of losing their love, of loving them too much, of losing them. The truth is that having a child is an act of perpetual masochism. . . at least for me. I've always been afraid.
ANA: You, afraid?
LAURA: Yes. A fear different from yours. You were always afraid of real things, but I've always feared the unknown. I was scared to death of the future. I'm still scared of it.
ANA: But you were always talking about your future. . . always planning things.
LAURA: Because of fear. I'd try to plan out a future before a different one snuck up on me. The only thing I like is the past. I can't understand the present and don't know how to manage in it. The past is the only thing I really have left. I hold on to it so tight. That's why it's so hard for me to let go of this house. . . of these memories. Because the best part about memories is that you can choose the ones to keep. And you always remember the good: my wedding day. . . the first time I breastfed Yoli. . . you and I when we were little, hiding up in the attic. . . the time we spent cutting out paper dolls. . . my son's first word. Did you know he didn't speak for the longest time? He was almost three. We thought he was mute. Those are the good things I have. . . the kinds of things you seem to put down and want me to forget. What I have now is useless. You see how Antonio uses and manipulates me. And what's worse he doesn't give a damn about me as a woman. He's not having an affair. At least that would be more bearable. Suspicions, jealousy, spite. . . something to think about. But that's not it. He's not involved with another woman. He just doesn't care about me. The kids. . . They're still my children, but they're not my babies anymore. I'm no longer afraid for them, just worried. Then there's the house. The worst part about the house is once you get it settled. When you're busy setting up, you barely have time to think about anything else.

But when it becomes your home, you realize that it's only good for company and for dusting. Your company flees their home after they've dusted and comes to see how you've dusted yours. You, in turn, become someone else's company and when you finish talking about dusting, you come home again. And you're still bored. Then you look for someone to do the housework and try to escape. You start the rounds of concerts and exhibits. . . not that they have any meaning for you. You're only interested in seeing who bought them same way you would check the price of hamburger meat at the store. Sometimes you go to the movies. . . But Spencer Tracy isn't there anymore. And if you see Liz Taylor, you realize she's fat and she's no longer that pretty young woman in white. And you ask yourself if the same thing is going to happen to you. Because men on the street don't turn their heads to look at you anymore. So you go straight to the beauty salon and they tug and pull at you and give you the same haircut every other woman on the street has and make you buy all those expensive wonder creams. Then you sit around waiting for that miracle in the mirror. But nothing happens. You still just see your plain old boring face staring back at you. And so you try working, but you don't know how to do anything, except be a housewife or embroider. You don't even know how to write a simple business letter. You aren't even sure how to spell. You don't know the proper heading or how to start the letter because what they taught you was already outdated. Then you go home again and try to entertain yourself watching over the people you hired to do the housework. You don't read because no one ever expected you to. And it's too late anyway because now there's television and all. Sometimes you get together with friends. It's great fun. You prepare a luncheon for a group and one of the women introduces a new cleaning product. Your friends order it and then you get a new Tupperware container or a yogurt maker, except the yogurt maker never works right. Then they leave. . . and you're alone again, waiting for your family to come home and tell you about their day. But they never share anything with you. They come home and they're tired and hungry. They watch television or listen to music with those little gadgets they stick in their ears. . . those gadgets that don't even let you listen to the music. Their music is only theirs. . . or they sleep. Everyone always sleeps at home. They sleep so effortlessly, while you have to down a ton a sleeping pills to get the same effect. And everyday is the same. You're home alone with the telephone. The phone is a primary necessity. You call all your friends and they always tell you the same stories. Or you call those talk shows on the radio. It's great fun, except the first thing they ask you to do is turn down the radio, which annoys you the most because if you're calling it's because you want to hear your voice. Other times it's always busy and by the time someone picks up, you already forgot why you called. But it really doesn't matter because you just talk away. That's the real reason you called anyway. And you call about the classified ads. You'd be surprised how many things people sell. Especially the number of wedding gowns... and houses too. They sell a whole bunch just like this one. Some are furnished, they even leave the paintings on the walls. That's what must happen when people die and no one is interested in keeping their things. Did you know that I still have my wedding dress? It had a twenty foot train. It's such a shame you couldn't come to my wedding. You sent me a telegram from...

ANA: Viña del Mar...

LAURA: That's it. Viña del Mar. I still remember what it said: Congratulations! You're getting married for the both of us. I've kept it all these years... Along with one of my wedding bouquet roses and one of Yoli's baby booties... In that Italian box of chocolates Aunt Susana gave us. Do you remember? She brought it from Rome when she went for the Pope's blessing. I'd recognize each and every thing in that box even with my eyes closed. I know exactly where your telegram is. I keep a lot of things there. I sit up many nights and review the contents of my little box of treasures. Everyone's asleep... and I drink. Maybe more than I should, but it helps... Helps me to remember all the good things that have happened to me in my life. I relive them, just like a movie rerun on television. You... Dad... our old dolls, they're all a part of my movie. Wait! *(She gets up quickly and pulls out an old doll from one of the boxes near the window. She sits down right there on the floor and shows it to her sister.)* Look! It's Holly Hobbie! Dressed as a housewife! Do you remember? She's missing an eye and some hair. We used to dress her and comb her hair. *(Rocks the doll in her arms.)* And we would sing her the songs we learned in school... *(She starts to hum, then sing, as the words start coming back to her.)*

This is the way we wash our clothes, wash our clothes, wash our clothes
This is the way we wash our clothes
So early in the morning...

(Ana has also gotten up and moved closer to where LAURA is. She takes the doll from LAURA while she sings. ANA and LAURA sing together.)

This is the way we dance and sing, dance and sign, dance and sing
This is the way we dance and sing
So early in the morning...

Packing up the Past-35

ANA *(Gets up and throws the doll across the room)*: Stop! I don't want to remember that song!

LAURA: But you haven't forgotten the words. You don't need to remember anything. It's in here. . . like me. . .

ANA: But remembering doesn't do any good. Those times are over. We're not little girls anymore. It's all a trap. Don't you realize how trapped you are?

LAURA: Of course I do! But I'm not like you! I don't know how to escape!

ANA: You have to leave all this crap behind! The only way you can do it is thinking! Use your brain for something besides watching reruns.

LAURA: I don't know how! I don't want to think because that way I don't have to deal with anything. I don't want to be aware of the fact that I'm rotting away. . . I know I'm dying inside, I don't need to think to know it's true. What I need are solutions! Do you have any? Well, then leave me the hell alone! Let me stay here being what I am or get me out of here. Don't give me your cheap philosophy. What have you gained? Are you happy? How are we different? Does your husband pay any more attention to you than mine pays me? What about your job? Is there a difference between dusting your own bookshelves and dusting someone else's? I want to see how you've changed. I still see a little girl who was scared stiff at night and would climb into bed with me when there was a storm. Even though you find it hard to admit, you're just as trapped as I am. We've shared the same ideas. Ideas that were instilled in us and that continue to drag us down. The only difference between us is the way we've tried to escape. We tried different methods, but they didn't work for either one of us. And it kills you to realize that this garbage ties you down you just as much as me. Because it's the only real thing we have in our lives.

ANA: No! *(She jumps up and starts ripping up papers and throwing things on the floor.)* Nothing ties me down! Damn it! To hell with it! It's all a bunch of crap!!

LAURA: Ripping it up doesn't accomplish anything. It's still there!

ANA *(Has stopped in front of her father's portrait)*: You! What are you doing there? Are you enjoying what you've created? *(Throws her drink at him,)* Omnipotent, as always. . . Giving us that sideways glance! You're the first thing we should be ripping up! *(Takes down the portrait and begins to hit it.)* You're the one to blame for everything! It's all your fault! You! With your pride! Your lack of caring!

LAURA *(Trying to intervene)*: No! Leave him alone! Not Daddy! Please! Not Daddy!

ANA: It's not Daddy! It's his damned portrait! Don't you realize that? Don't hit me! Hit him! He's the one who started the destruction of our lives! He's the one you have to hit! Come on. . . hit him! *(She takes LAURA's hand and*

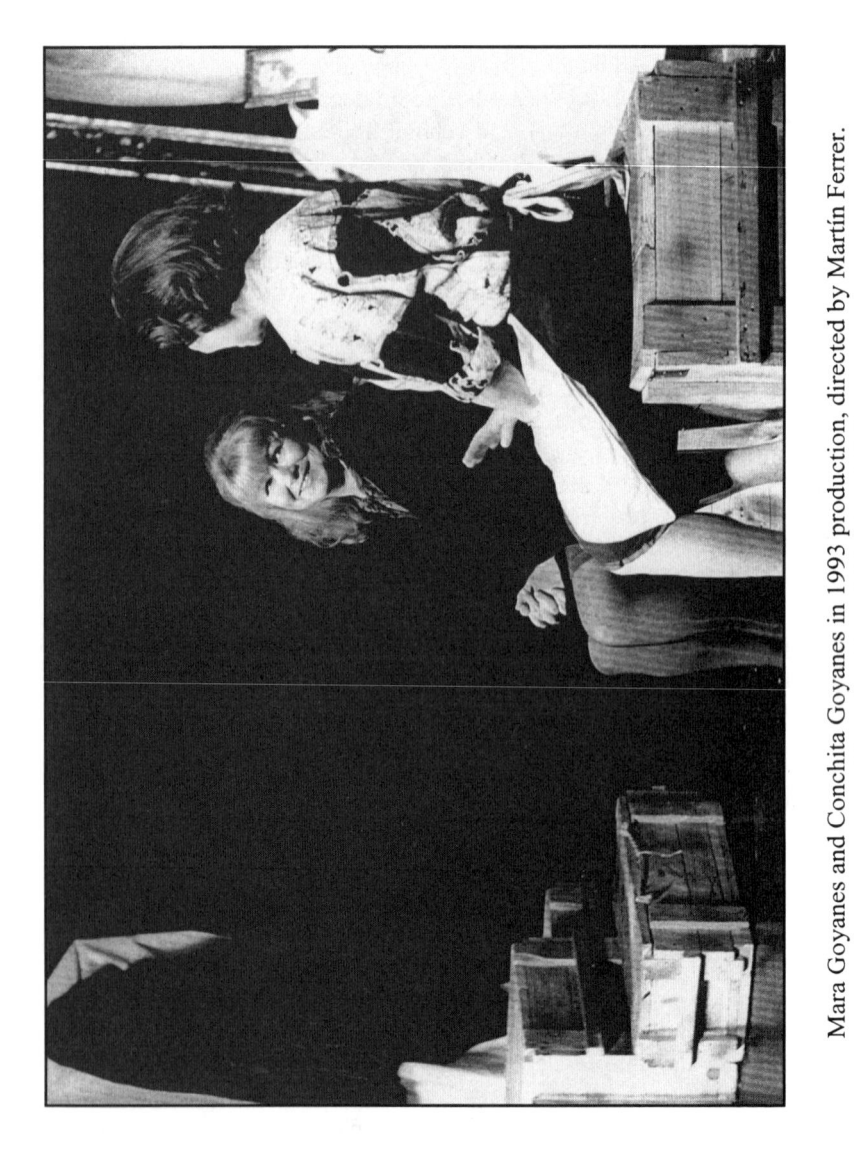

Mara Goyanes and Conchita Goyanes in 1993 production, directed by Martín Ferrer. Photo by Manuel Martínez Muñoz.

Packing up the Past-37

forces her to hit the portrait.) Hit him! For everything he stole from us! Hit him! For his lies! Good! Remember his belt! It didn't hurt him when he hit us! Come on, now! Harder! Remember when he used to lock us up!
LAURA: Daddy!...Da...
ANA: He didn't love you! He never loved us! He only loved himself! Come on, be brave! Now it's your turn! He never loved us, Laura! He hasn't allowed us to love! LAURA: Damn you! Damn you! Damn...*(She starts to bang hysterically on the portrait, until she is exhausted.)* Damn you ! Damn you!
ANA *(Holds her on her lap and rocks her)*: Easy, easy. Calm down! You finally did it! We've done it! Easy... Easy. *(Hums her a tune.)* Cry... Cry if you want... Easy... *(She slowly helps LAURA get herself together, sits her up, pours her a drink and gives it to her.)* Drink it, it'll do you some good. *(ANA starts picking up some of the papers she threw around earlier and puts some things back where they belong.)*
LAURA: I really shouldn't drink anymore... I'm very drunk. Look what I did.
ANA: You did what you should have done a long time ago. That's all. When it comes down to it, it was only a damned portrait. And brace yourself... We've just begun. So far we've only done the hardest part. It's got to be easier from here on in. It's not worth all this anger. We should be having fun. It's a fact that we have to divide up our inheritance, but I can assure you we'll have a good time in the process. Nothing is worth so much pain. Besides, we can't destroy everything. After all, these things are valuable. And both of us are here for the money. At least that's why we've been forced to come. *(She sits next to LAURA.)* Think! There must be a way to divide this without any more suffering. Think!
LAURA: I'm sorry, but I have too many drinks in me to think. Besides, who cares anyway? Having to divide things up is unpleasant in and of itself.
ANA: It wouldn't be if we made fun of the whole thing. We have to think of something to ridicule the entire situation... I've got it! Do you have a deck of cards?
LAURA: A deck of cards?
ANA *(Starts looking through the boxes)*: Yeah, a deck of cards... Some dice. Something like that. I thought I saw a game of Parcheesi around here somewhere...
LAURA: What are you doing?
ANA: You mean what are we doing. I'll tell you what we're doing. We're going to gamble for our inheritance!
LAURA: Are you crazy? We can't do that!
ANA: Of course we can! It's our inheritance. We can do what we want with it. Give it away, throw it way, gamble it away. I think it's the best solution. You and I are supposed to share and share alike. And according to you

that's not fair, right? Well, then let's play. We'll let fate decide and that way you and I will be on the sidelines. What do you think? Look, here are some dice. Should we play everything for the highest roll?

LAURA: I think it's crazy. It's like... It's like committing a sacrilege...

ANA: Don't be ridiculous... Be daring. I promise you God will not send punishment down from the heavens. *(Takes the list of jewelry.)* First lot: diamond engagement ring, white gold and diamond bracelet. Who rolls first?

LAURA: No... I don't want to. It's Mother's jewelry...

ANA: Forget what it is. In order to play and have a good time you can't think about what you're actually playing for. Think only of the game itself. Remember when we used to play poker with beans for chips? Well, these are our beans now. Come on! Think of Aunt Susana. Could you imagine her face if she saw us gambling for the family heirlooms?

LAURA *(Smiling)*: It would have been too much for her.

ANA: See? We can have fun with it. First lot... should you roll or should I?

LAURA *(Takes the dice from her)*: Let me try!

ANA: Bravo!

LAURA: Come on, dice! I want that bracelet! A four! Your turn!

ANA: Here I go! A one! Now that the first lot has been decided, it will go to my dear niece Yolanda! Next... Wait, I'm going to light some candles, it's getting dark. Here, you can start lighting this one. *(She hands her a candle and matches. She then brings another candle, lights it, puts it near where they are sitting, and sits down again.)* Second lot: Wed...

LAURA: Maybe it would be better if you didn't read it.

ANA: We have to read it. It wouldn't be any fun if we didn't. Wedding bands. Thirteen gold dowry coins, gold charm bracelet. Have I ever seen that one before?

LAURA: Yes, of course you have... the one with the little jade buddhas. Now it's your turn.

ANA: A six! Looks like I get the bangles and the buddhas...

LAURA: A four! That must be my number.

ANA: Well, now we're tied. Don't worry, I'll let you borrow the coins when Yolanda gets married.

LAURA *(Reading)*: Third lot: sapphire earrings with matching ring. I always liked them a lot. Should I roll?

ANA: Go ahead. If Antonio could only see us now!

LAURA: I'll bet you it would give him another ulcer. A five! Your turn! Another five! We'll have to roll again, this lot can't be divided up.

ANA: Here goes! A three!

LAURA: Let's see if I can get higher... A five! They're mine!

Packing up the Past-39

ANA: Fourth lot. At this rate we'll be done in no time! A pair of pearl earrings with a matching necklace, and seven gold bangle bracelets. Who rolls? Me?
LAURA: Why not? You know, I'm starting to have fun time with this. *(She pours herself some more cognac.)*
ANA: You should stop drinking. Maybe tomorrow, when you're sober, you'll regret this.
LAURA: Of course I will! But right now I'm having fun and I don't care about anything.
ANA: If you want, we can stop playing. . .
LAURA: No way! What's wrong? Are you starting to regret this?
ANA: No, but maybe you're right. Maybe we don't have the right to divide up our inheritance like this.
LAURA: First you convince me, then you make me play, and now you're the one who's having second thoughts. . . Roll!
ANA: Fine. If you're sure. . . A five!
LAURA: A two! It's yours! Fifth lot: gold bracelets, chains and medals. My turn. A three! I guess today's not my lucky day.
ANA: A two! Hey, maybe it is! Sixth lot: gold watch, man's gold ring with ruby. . . It was Father's.
LAURA: And Dad's watch. . . Roll! A four! I have to get higher!
ANA: I wish you would. I really don't want this one.
LAURA: Too bad. . . it's yours. I only got a two. What's next?
ANA: Listen, Laura. . . if you want, we can just forget this. Luck isn't on your side and I feel guilty. Maybe I really don't have a right to anything.
LAURA: A game is a game! Forget your silly scruples. What roll is this?
ANA: Seventh: emerald ring and brooch. I've never seen them.
LAURA: They're the last gift Dad gave her. My turn. A five. . .
ANA: A three!
LAURA: You see? My luck is changing.
ANA: Lot eight: gold earrings with semiprecious stones. Your turn.
LAURA: No, it's your turn.
ANA: A six.
LAURA: A two.
ANA: Ninth: platinum earrings, ring and brooch.
LAURA: Three!
ANA: Five!
LAURA *(Reading)*: It seems we're almost done with the jewelry. Lot ten: silver necklaces, rings, brooches and bracelets. A silver rosary. Do you remember it? When Dad said he was buying it for Mother, we went in on it with him.
ANA: For a grand total of one dollar.

LAURA: And forty seven cents. We had a lot of pennies in our piggy bank. Lot ten: silver necklaces, rings, bracelets and rosary, the latter with an appraised value of one dollar and forty-seven cents... Roll!
ANA: Let's stop. That's enough. The important part is to prove to ourselves we could gamble for all of it.
LAURA: If we want to prove that to ourselves, we have to go all the way. Hurry up, there are still some things left and you have to leave for Madrid soon. You can't miss the train.
ANA: It's still early. It's just that it gets dark earlier in the winter.
LAURA: It doesn't matter. We have to finish this once and for all.
ANA: But tomorrow...
LAURA: Tomorrow doesn't matter. Right now is what's important. Tomorrow you won't be here... Maybe we won't see each other for several years. I'll be sober and have to give Antonio a convincing explanation... but it'll be too late. He'll have to deal with the outcome. Let's finish as soon as possible. Roll!
ANA: Two!
LAURA: Six! That's it! What's next?
ANA: In this lot, there are a number of silver pieces: ashtrays, trays, a coffee set and a tea set. Your turn.
LAURA: A five!
ANA: One!
LAURA: Come on! What's next? I'm on a roll now!
ANA: Lot twelve: two sets of sterling silverware. A three!
LAURA: A four! I guess that's mine too. I'm going to end up saving my husband money. That's the only thing that bothers me.
ANA: That just goes to show you how stupid gambling is. What are you laughing about? Are you having fun?
LAURA: Just because I'm laughing, doesn't mean I'm having fun. I'm laughing because it's funny that you're stuck with Father's ring and watch. You can't tell me it's not comical. Plus, I'm laughing because this is all such a surprise. I didn't think I'd be brave enough to go through with it, and I'm nervous, so I laugh. *(Reads.)* Lot thirteen: three autographed paintings and several watercolors. *(Looks at the portrait.)* Well, I guess I should say two autographed portraits and several watercolors. Do you want to go first or should I?
ANA: I will. Let's get this over with! A four!
LAURA: Another four! Come on, we have to break the tie.
ANA: Another four! That makes three in a row!
LAURA: A three! Now you have something to decorate the house with.

ANA: They'll come in handy, even though I never really liked the watercolors. I don't think there are any more lots. This is the last one: bronze ink stand and two fifteenth-century manuscripts.
LAURA: Oh yes, those old texts Dad venerated so. They're supposedly worth quite a bit of money nowadays.
ANA: I can see. You roll, it's your turn.
LAURA: Five!
ANA: One! They're yours.
LAURA: Good. I always liked Dad's ink stand, with those twisted eagles on it.
ANA: Well, we're done. . . Finally!
LAURA: We're not finished yet. There's the house.
ANA: No. We can't gamble the house.
LAURA: Why not? We decided we would gamble for all of it, regardless of its value. What's wrong? Does the house mean as much to you as the jewelry does to me? Are you scared?
ANA: I'm sorry. The house represents a large sum of money, and I need it. I can't allow myself to play any more games.
LAURA: But if you win the house, all the money will be yours.
ANA: But I could lose. . . and I can't afford that luxury. I'd rather accept Antonio's offer. It's more sensible.
LAURA: If you regret playing the game, we can forget the whole thing. You can recuperate the third for the jewelry plus your half of the house.
ANA: No, that's okay. We gambled and that's that. Let's not talk about it anymore. As for the house, we'll do what Antonio suggested. It's more sensible.
LAURA: Okay. Whatever you say. What about the rest?
ANA: What's left?
LAURA: There's furniture, household things, sets of dishes. . . They might be useful to you.
ANA: Yes, maybe. . . but it's so late already. Anyway, I'd have to talk it over with Carlos.
LAURA: A lot of these things are useless to me. If you want, you can stay here tonight and we'll finish taking care of everything tomorrow. Or you could come another day.
ANA: No. I'd rather finish today. Now. Look. . . that table over there. If you don't need it, I could use it. And some curtains. . . and I could use some chairs. When you think about it, the truth is I only have a couple of armchairs and a bed. I could use anything that would help me furnish a two-room apartment. You pick it out and send me what you want.
LAURA: Aren't you taking anything now?

ANA: No. Well maybe I'll just take the shepherd painting. *(She gets up and wraps it.)* Yes, I'll take it with me. I should get going if I don't want to miss the last train.
LAURA: You should stay.
ANA: No, I can't. And you? What are you going to do?
LAURA: When you leave, I'm going to bed. I think I went a little overboard with the drinking.
ANA: You're going to sleep here? With no light?
LAURA: I have candles. Besides, I always sleep with the light off. What's the difference?
ANA: I. . . I still sleep with the light on. Me and my fear. I can't believe you're brave enough to stay here alone tonight. I'd never be able to do it.
LAURA: I'm not that happy about it either, but I'm alone. . . you're leaving. I'm used to being alone. Tomorrow I'll pick up a little around here and then I'll go home.
ANA: Why don't you come with me now? We could make the trip together. . .
LAURA: No. I have to stay. I have a lot of things to take care of here. But I'd like you to stay. It would be our last night here together.
ANA: I'm sorry, but I'm just not up to it. Besides, this afternoon has already been plenty. . . too many emotions in such a short time. I'm sorry I'm leaving..
LAURA: That's okay, I'm used to it. I'll probably fall asleep right away with everything I've drunk. But I would have liked to see you tomorrow morning. . . with both of us more alert.
ANA: It would be like this afternoon when we first saw each other. We would treat each other like strangers.
LAURA: No. That won't happen to us again. This afternoon must have been good for something.
ANA: For us to realize that nothing changes. . . not us. . . not our lives. We're the same ignorant, scared little girls that played in this house. We've only gained in years and disillusionment. We'll both try to forget this afternoon. It'll always be the afternoon we packed up the house.
LAURA *(Looks at her surroundings sarcastically)*: You mean the afternoon we destroyed it. That's what we've really done.
ANA: But it doesn't matter. We did it with our hands. Everything that is in this house will always still be here. *(Pointing to her head.)* Not even here. *(Pointing to her heart.)* And I know that whatever happens, it will always be that way.
LAURA: Always. . . is such a long time. . .
ANA: It depends. . . sometimes it's too short.

Packing up the Past-43

LAURA: I was convinced... I was sure... That you... At least you would have gotten what you wanted. Without being a doctor. Without winning the Nobel Prize... By being far away from here. I thought you would be able to escape.
ANA: As you can see, you were wrong. I'm here. I've traveled. I've tried to escape. But here I am... Just like you... Or even worse, who knows? It's hard to change. We're just like rag dolls. All the same. One after another. The only thing that makes dolls different is their outfit and hair. But everything else is the same. They last forever, they're hard to break, but it's no use hiding their identity. Everyone knows who they are. And when you compare them to the dolls they have nowadays... The plastic ones, the ones that walk, talk, and even have genitals... When you compare you realize they're outdated. They don't fit in. Holly Hobbies need old-fashioned doll houses and pretty lace and bows and metal toy soldiers and wooden horses and cars. They only look right around those kinds of things. Put them next to anything else and they look ridiculous, obsolete, useless.
LAURA: You think that if we were boys everything would have been different.
ANA: Maybe we'd be happier. Men have a greater capacity to adapt. We only know how to adapt our bodies. They have more practice and have learned to adapt their minds.
ANA: It's all the same, Laura... the same. We each make what we want of our lives. *(She gets up, puts on her coat and gets her bag and the painting. She then crosses to her sister and kisses her.)* Bye... I have to go. Are you sure you're not coming?
LAURA *(Gets up and gets the candle holder)*: Yes. I'll walk you to the door. Is that all you're taking with you?
ANA *(Remembering)*: No, I have something else. *(She takes out the pieces of the picture she had ripped up and shows them to her sister.)*
LAURA: Your school picture!
ANA: You see, when it comes down to it, I like collecting memories too. It'll be a puzzle on my trip. Get to bed soon. You look tired.
LAURA: Yes. Let me call home and then I'll go to sleep. Will I see you soon?
ANA: Yes... Soon. We'll call each other. I want to see the kids. *(Already at the door.)* Go to bed, it's very cold.
LAURA: Yes. I'll call you. As soon as things are underway, I'll call you. Take care of yourself. Bye.
ANA: Good-bye. You can close the door, there's light in the stairway. *(Exits.)*
LAURA: Good-bye... *(She watches her leave in silence, then turns around and closes the door. She looks at the curtains, moves near them and stares out the window. She sees her sister step out to the street and goes to wave to her, but stops. We assume her sister hasn't looked back. She watches ANA*

leave, then slowly draws the curtains and crosses to the phone. She picks up the phone and goes to dial, but hangs it up again. Finally, she decides to call and dials.) Emilia? It's Mrs. Castillo again. Is my husband home? The kids? Did you tell my husband I called? And he didn't leave a message? Very well, then. When he gets back let him know. . . Actually don't tell him anything. I'll call him. . . No, I don't want them calling me. . . I'm going to bed right now. Yes. It's the same migraine I always get. It's making me have a horrible afternoon. . . Thank you, Emilia. Oh! Tomorrow morning please buy something to roast. The Gonzalez's are coming over for dinner. I'll see you tomorrow. . . I don't know what time I'll be home. . . No, don't say anything to them. . . Thank you, Emilia. . . Goodnight.

(She hangs up and goes to walk out when she remembers her drink and the bottle of cognac. She picks them up and is about to walk out again when she stumbles over something. It's part of her father's portrait, which she picks up. She places the candelabrum on the floor and kneels to gather the pieces. Little by little she gathers the pieces and stretches the canvas of the painting. She begins cleaning the portrait with the corner of her blouse. She does so slowly and carefully. Her movements are mechanical, slow. The curtain also falls slowly.)

THE END

CRITICAL REACTION TO THE PLAY

"Sebastián Junyent, a talented author, provides two magnificent actresses--Amparo Rivelles and Lola Cardona--with the opportunity to reveal their great skill in an open, verbal game, filled with tension and contrast. The result is an admirable performance (running for hundreds of performances in Madrid and on tour throughout Spain) that was awarded a double prize for best actress of 1985."

Francisco Álvaro
El Espectador y la Crítica (Spain, 1986)

"Junyent explores "the motivations for feminine behavior: the influence that the family has on women, the emotional force of memory, the permanent conflict between reality and dreams, between desires and fears, a certain inability to really live freedom..."

Lorenzo López Sancho
ABC (Madrid, January 1985)

"The text also touches on the problems of a society in transition, memories attributable to life under Francoism, the disarray of women in their forties facing the balance sheet of their education."

Laure Bernard
Le Figaro (France, July 1991)

"This is a surprisingly well-made bourgeois drama. With fine theatrical effect, it goes from the comic to the dramatic. Its finely-tuned dialogues give rise to what could be called a stage dual, marvelously interpreted by two of our best actresses..."

Myrna Lluch
El Vocero (San Juan, November 1987)

"In general, great dramas are far removed from the possibilities of common mortals. In general, we are called upon to fight the little things, the small, insubstantial pebbles we find in our path; but that is also the tragedy of these two women. They are obliged to fight against a dull gray life, filled with permanent frustrations. It is a life that weighs upon the very center of their being. From their painful, joint confession, we learn just how much they hate it."

Santiago Aizarna
El Diario Vasco (San Sebastián, August 1985)

ABOUT THE TRANSLATOR

Born in Valladolid, Spain and raised in Orange County, New York, Ana Mengual is a 1991 graduate of the State University of New York-Binghamton where she majored in Spanish and History, took courses in French and Italian, and began her study of translation. She subsequently earned a Master of Arts in Spanish (Translation Option) at Rutgers, The State University of New Jersey, where she worked on a variety of translations, with emphasis on literary and business texts. Her internship assignment while at Rutgers in the legal department of Banco Santander in New York led to several years of employment in that Spanish bank as a translator specializing in legal and financial documents. In May 1999, she received an MBA degree from the Stern School of Business at New York University and is currently employed by Chase Manhattan Bank in New York.

TRANSLATOR'S ACKNOWLEDGMENTS

I would like to dedicate this translation to my parents for the encouragement they have always given me and the love of foreign languages they have instilled. I wish to express my gratitude to Phyllis Zatlin for her guidance during my time of study at Rutgers and for her active interest in publishing the present translation. My thanks as well to Margrette Brown and Leonardo Mazzara for their assistance in the preparation of this edition and to the Program for Cultural Cooperation between Spain's Ministry of Education and Culture and United States' Universities for their generous support.

A.M.

ESTRENO: CONTEMPORARY SPANISH PLAYS SERIES
General Editor: Phyllis Zatlin

No. 1   Jaime Salom: ***Bonfire at Dawn*** *(Una hoguera al amanecer)*
Translated by Phyllis Zatlin. 1992.
ISBN: 0-9631212-0-0

No. 2   José López Rubio: ***In August We Play the Pyrenees*** *(Celos del aire)*
Translated by Marion Peter Holt. 1992.
ISBN: 0-9631212-1-9

No. 3   Ramón del Valle-Inclán: ***Savage Acts: Four Plays*** *(Ligazón, La rosa de papel, La cabeza del Bautista, Sacrilegio)*
Translated by Robert Lima. 1993.
ISBN: 0-9631212-2-7

No. 4   Antonio Gala: ***The Bells of Orleans*** *(Los buenos días perdidos)*
Translated by Edward Borsoi. 1993.
ISBN: 0-9631212-3-5

No. 5   Antonio Buero-Vallejo: ***The Music Window*** *(Música cercana)*
Translated by Marion Peter Holt. 1994.
ISBN: 0-9631212-4-3

No. 6   Paloma Pedrero: ***Parting Gestures with A Night in the Subway*** *(El color de agosto, La noche dividida, Resguardo personal, Solos esta noche)*
Translated by Phyllis Zatlin. Revised edition. 1999.
ISBN: 1-888463-06-6

No. 7   Ana Diosdado: ***Yours for the Asking*** *(Usted también podrá disfrutar de ella)*
Translated by Patricia W. O'Connor. 1995.
ISBN: 0-9631212-6-X

No. 8   Manuel Martínez Mediero: ***A Love Too Beautiful*** *(Juana del amor hermoso)*
Translated by Hazel Cazorla. 1995.
ISBN: 0-9631212-7-8

No. 9   Alfonso Vallejo: ***Train to Kiu*** *(El cero transparente)*
Translated by H. Rick Hite. 1996.
ISBN: 0-9631212-8-6

No. 10   Alfonso Sastre: ***The Abandoned Doll. Young Billy Tell.*** *(Historia de una muñeca abandonada. El único hijo de William Tell)*
Translated by Carys Evans-Corrales. 1996.
ISBN: 1-888463-00-7

No. 11   Lauro Olmo and Pilar Enciso: *The Lion Calls a Meeting.The Lion Foiled.*
         The Lion in Love. (*Asamblea general. Los leones*)
         Translated by Carys Evans-Corrales. 1997.
         ISBN: 1-888463-01-5

No. 12   José Luis Alonso de Santos: *Hostages in the Barrio.* (*La estanquera de Vallecas*)
         Translated by Phyllis Zatlin. 1997.
         ISBN: 1-888463-02-3

No. 13   Fermín Cabal: *Passage.* (*Travesía*)
         Translated by H. Rick Hite. 1998.
         ISBN: 1-888463-03-1

No. 14   Antonio Buero-Vallejo: *The Sleep of Reason* (*El sueño de la razón*)
         Translated by Marion Peter Holt. 1998.
         ISBN: 1-888463-04-X

No. 15   Fernando Arrabal: *The Body-Builder's Book of Love* (*Breviario de amor de un halterófilo*)
         Translated by Lorenzo Mans. 1999.
         ISBN: 1-888463-05-8

No. 16   Luis Araújo: *Vanzetti.* (*Vanzetti*)
         Translated by Mary Alice Lessing. 1999.
         ISBN: 1-888463-08-2

No. 17   Josep M. Benet I Jornet: *Legacy.* (*Testament*)
         Translated by Janet DeCesaris. 2000.
         ISBN: 1-888463-09-0

No. 18   Sebastián Junyent: *Packing up the Past.* (*Hay que deshacer la casa*)
         Translated by Ana Mengual. 2000.
         ISBN: 1-888463-10-4

ORDER FORM

List price, nos. 1-11: $6; revised ed. no. 6 and nos. 12-18, $8.
Shipping and handling for one or two volumes, $1.25 each.
Free postage on orders of three or more volumes.
Special price for complete set of 18 volumes, $90.

Please indicate below quantities and titles of plays: TOTAL

___ _____   _____
___ _____   _____
___ _____   _____
___ _____   _____
___ _____   _____
___ _____   _____

                    Shipping & handling   _____

                    AMOUNT ENCLOSED   _____

Name and address: _____

                    _____

                    _____

Make checks payable to ESTRENO Plays and send to:

ESTRENO Plays
Dept. of Spanish & Portuguese, FAS
Rutgers, The State University of New Jersey
105 George St.
New Brunswick, NJ 08901-1414

For information on discounts available to bookstores, contact:
FAX: 1-732/ 932-9837   Phone: 1-732/932-9412x25
E-mail: ESTRPLAY@rci.rutgers.edu
Visit our web page: www.rci.rutgers.edu/~estrplay/webpage.html